T0277918

FRANK LLOYD WRIGHT'S
WISCONSIN

FRANK LLOYD WRIGHT'S
WISCONSIN

How America's Most Famous Architect
Found Inspiration in His Home State

Kristine Hansen

Globe
Pequot

Essex, Connecticut

Globe Pequot

An imprint of Globe Pequot, the trade division of
The Rowman & Littlefield Publishing Group, Inc.
4501 Forbes Blvd., Ste. 200
Lanham, MD 20706
www.rowman.com

Distributed by NATIONAL BOOK NETWORK

Copyright © 2023 by Kristine Hansen

All rights reserved. No part of this book may be reproduced in any form or by any electronic or mechanical means, including information storage and retrieval systems, without written permission from the publisher, except by a reviewer who may quote passages in a review.

British Library Cataloguing in Publication Information available

Library of Congress Cataloging-in-Publication Data
Names: Hansen, Kristine, author.
Title: Frank Lloyd Wright's Wisconsin : how America's most famous architect
    found inspiration in his home state / Kristine Hansen.
Description: Essex, Connecticut : Globe Pequot, [2023] | Includes index. |
    Summary: "A comprehensive guide to Wright's designs (and those of his
    protégés) that are open to the public—as well as insider historical
    information about sites now demolished, and those available for
    'drive-bys' only. For architecture or history fans looking for tours,
    overnight stays, or creative inspiration. Museum collections in
    Wisconsin that include Wright's furnishings and drawings are also
    included"— Provided by publisher.
Identifiers: LCCN 2022044382 (print) | LCCN 2022044383 (ebook) | ISBN
    9781493069149 (paperback) | ISBN 9781493069156 (epub)
Subjects: LCSH: Wright, Frank Lloyd, 1867–1959—Homes and
    haunts—Wisconsin—Guidebooks. | Wright, Frank Lloyd, 1867–1959—Friends
    and associates. | Architecture—Wisconsin—Guidebooks. |
    Wisconsin—Guidebooks.
Classification: LCC NA737.W7 H325 2023 (print) | LCC NA737.W7 (ebook) |
    DDC 720.92—dc23/eng/20220920
LC record available at https://lccn.loc.gov/2022044382
LC ebook record available at https://lccn.loc.gov/2022044383

∞™ The paper used in this publication meets the minimum requirements of American National Standard for Information Sciences—Permanence of Paper for Printed Library Materials, ANSI/NISO Z39.48-1992.

CONTENTS

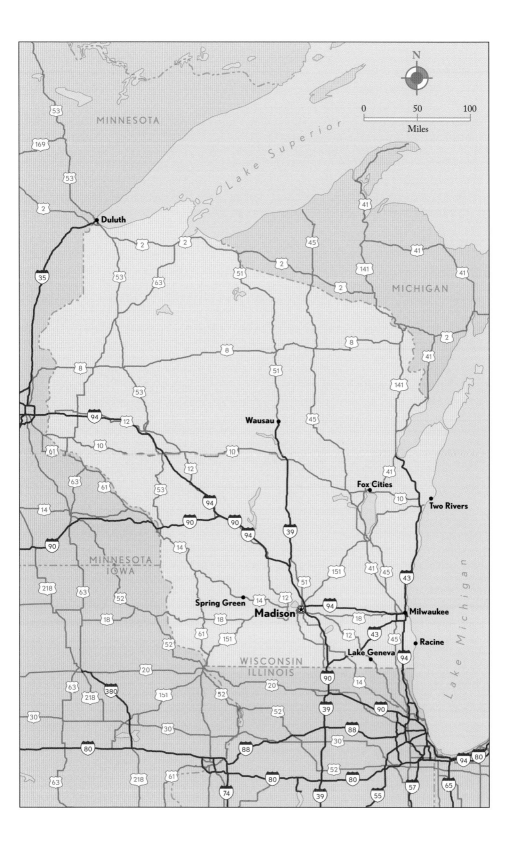

INTRODUCTION

Who was Frank Lloyd Wright?

I was with friends at a Friday fish fry—if you don't know, this is a very Wisconsin tradition—when someone posed this question. It was then that I realized most people connect Wright with his architectural projects but not necessarily his character and personality.

As a journalist I make a career out of picking up the phone and interviewing people who are still living. But in writing this book, I grappled with the legacy of the deceased. Stories from those who knew Wright during the time he was alive are the only living pieces of the puzzle. And as Wright died in 1959, the number of people who once stood in the same room with him is dwindling. These stories are now on the second or third generation, with descendants of those who commissioned his designs left to bare the truth.

Still, there are commonalities within these stories. Wright was charismatic. He could woo families into commissioning one of his designs and handing over all of the decorative decisions to him. If you wanted a Wright house you bought into his design, not yours. While on a visit to Wingspread, Irene Purcell Johnson was startled to wake up and see Wright had rearranged all of the artwork and furnishings overnight. (He was never invited back. Or, he never came back. We'll never know the reason.) In another story, Wright was invited to lunch at the Willard Keland House and found the piano to be "in the wrong place." Even Margaret Howland, whose family owns the Frederick C. Bogk House in Milwaukee, commented during our interview that she found it impossible to rearrange the furnishings in her childhood bedroom. It was that unchangeable. Another fun story comes from the Hardy House, where onetime owner Peterkin Seward declared that everything in the home was built to Wright's height, and not hers. As she wrote to Mark Hertzberg, author of a comprehensive book on the Hardy House that was published in 2006 (*Frank Lloyd Wright's Hardy House*, Pomegranate Books), "It was the most miserable kitchen to work in. The counters were Wright's height. The height of the counters was wrong."

Yet despite a lack of collaboration with the client, Wright clearly possessed talent. According to the Frank Lloyd Wright Foundation, he designed 1,114 structures, of which 532 were built, over a period of seventy years. Of those, 432 are still standing. And, of the eight that were placed on the list of UNESCO World Heritage Sites in 2008, two are in Wisconsin: the Herbert and Katherine Jacobs House I in Madison, and Taliesin, Wright's Spring Green homestead. In this book I use "built" to imply completion dates.

As a relative of mine said, he was "the prophet of the new." There are many firsts in Wright's designs, with radiant floor heating among them. When his first homes were built, in the late 1800s, in what is now the Frank Lloyd Wright Historic District in Oak Park, Illinois, American streets were decorated with rambling Victorians, their turrets and gingerbread trim a nod to craftsmanship. The concept of *organic architecture*—a term attached to Wright, meaning that the outside is seamlessly brought into the interior spaces through natural light and intentional choices for building materials—was a stark contrast to cramped rooms with high ceilings and scant light. Wright skillfully managed to put his own imprint in the neighborhood while also riffing on those designs. The homes that still remain are definitely rambling and span multiple levels, but also introduce concepts like a concealed front door on the side of the house, not the front, and multiple built-ins that maximize storage while maintaining a fuss-free interior.

Despite this eventual success, Wright lived under a cloud of pressure from a very young age. He was only a child when his mother Anna declared he would become a successful architect. How does a person even begin to entertain other fields of study and careers with this expectation? Could it be that she recognized his talent at such a young age?

Those who commissioned one of his designs not only wanted to live in the house, they longed to be associated with him. Bernard Schwartz—commissioner of a home in Two Rivers, Wisconsin, in 1940—even began to emulate his attire, much to the dismay of his wife, by donning a top hat and cape. Another theme: Wright's works were always over budget. Craig Adelman, the second-generation owner of the Albert and Edith Adelman House in Fox Point, remembers as a child a man in a tall hat always asking his parents for more money.

"He was among the first to understand branding," said a tour guide at Taliesin, referring not only to Wright's architectural works, but also his flamboyant look with the cape, top hat, and cane. "He was driven to be successful and be in the public eye."

The Wisconsin commissions for private homes fall during two favorable times in Wright's career: 1902–1917 and 1937–1959. Those earlier homes embody Prairie-style and four-square architecture, a reaction to Victorian homes, while many of the later designs represent the Usonian period. When you walk through these homes today, it's clear that the Midcentury Modern design period made so popular with throwback shows like AMC's *Mad Men* (2007–2015) is woven into these homes, but with Wright's signature twists. Yes, there are floor-to-ceiling windows and stone fireplaces, but the kitchens lack an open layout. They are mostly galley-style, thought to be this way because Wright wasn't a cook himself. But he did love to eat and entertain, which is why the living rooms and communal spaces in his homes are expansive. The bedrooms? Not so much. Bedrooms were for sleeping, he suggested, and not hanging out away from the family. Could it be that because Wright grew up among many family members on a massive estate in Spring Green, Wisconsin, he naturally felt comfortable in a room with many others?

We do know he slept very few hours each night, which is why when you visit both Taliesin and Taliesin West, you will note that he and his third wife Olgivanna had separate bedrooms. When the muse strikes, you want to be in the drafting room, of course, and not disturb your partner each time you wake.

Another contribution from Wright are the many Japanese woodblock prints he brought back from Japan after his first trip in 1905. When I toured Burnham Block on Milwaukee's South Side, toward the end of the interview, curator Michael Lilek suggested that Wright may even be responsible for the collections in American museums today. One example is at the Museum of Fine Arts Boston, which houses the largest (and finest) collection of Japanese art outside of Japan. Though you won't find his name on the label next to a work, and they were gifted to the museum by other collectors, we now know he was the first curator.

Commentary about Wright must also include his quirks and nuances. He was relatively short for that time—5-foot-7—and had a distaste for tall people, viewing it as "wasted space." In *New World Odyssey: Annunciation Greek Orthodox Church and Frank Lloyd Wright*, author John Gurda narrates an experience from parishioner Stanley Stacy, who took Wright to dinner at the Wisconsin Club. He reportedly ate so many corn muffins the staff gave him a bag full to take home.

He loved to eat, but cooking? Not so much. His kitchens received many critiques for the cramped conditions, perhaps because Wright himself didn't spend much time in front of a stove. He also disliked designing swimming pools and basements, and did not have a soft spot for dogs, although in 1956 he did design "Eddie's Doghouse" for the Berger family (clients in San Anselmo, California), so their Labrador retriever Eddie could take cover during rain or inclement weather. It's on permanent display at the Marin County Civic Center in Marin County, California, another of Wright's buildings. Wright fans should not be surprised that this 4-square-foot mini home features a sloped roof—and it leaks.

TIMELINE OF FRANK LLOYD WRIGHT IN WISCONSIN

1863:   Wright's grandparents (Richard and Mallie Lloyd Jones) purchase land along the Wisconsin River near Spring Green

1867:   Born in Richland Center to Anna Lloyd Jones and William Carey Wright

1884:   Parents' divorce

1885:   Father moves away from Wisconsin

1885:   Worked in the office of Alan D. Conover

1886:   Admitted to the University of Wisconsin–Madison as a special student

1886:   Collaborated with Chicago architect Joseph Lyman Silsbee on Unity Chapel at Taliesin

1887:   Hillside Home School I built for Wright's aunts (Jane and Nell, who were teachers)

1889:   Married Catherine "Kitty" Wright

1890:   Son Frank Lloyd Wright Jr. born

1892:   Son John born

1893:   Robert M. Lamp Cottage ("Rocky Roost") built in Madison

1893:   Lake Mendota Boathouse built in Madison

1894:   Daughter Catherine born

1895:   Son David born

1897:   Romeo and Juliet Windmill built

1898:   Daughter Frances born

1900:   Henry Wallis Cottage built in Delavan

1900–03: Fred B. Jones Estate ("Penwern") built in Delavan

1902:   Delavan Lake Yacht Club built in Delavan

1902:   George W. Spencer House built in Delavan

1902:   Charles S. Ross House built in Delavan

1903:   Hillside Home School II built at Taliesin

1903:   Son Robert ("Llewelyn") born

1905:   Robert M. Lamp House built in Madison

1905:   A. P. Johnson House built in Delavan

1905:   Thomas P. Hardy House built in Racine

1907–08: Tan-Y-Deri House ("Andrew T. Porter House") built at Taliesin for sister Jane and her husband Andrew

1908:   Eugene A. Gilmore House built in Madison

1911:   Taliesin is started in Spring Green

1912:   The Geneva Inn is built in Lake Geneva

1912:   Observation platform built at Island Woolen Mills in Baraboo

1914:   Women's Building at Inter-County Fairgrounds built in Spring Green

1914:   Taliesin servant kills his mistress Mamah Borthwick and her two children, along with a draftsman, workman, and workman's son, setting a fire and murdering them with an ax; living quarters are destroyed and gardener dies from fire injuries

1915:   Delavan Lake Yacht Club demolished

1915:   Hillside Home School at Taliesin closes

1915:   Arthur L. Richards Bungalow ("Burnham Block") built in Milwaukee

1916:   Arthur L. Richards Duplex Apartments ("Burnham Block") built in Milwaukee

1916:   Arthur R. Munkwitz Duplex Apartments built in Milwaukee

1916:   Arthur L. Richards Small House ("Burnham Block") built in Milwaukee

1917:   Frederick C. Bogk House built in Milwaukee

1917:   Stephen M. B. Hunt II House built in Oshkosh

1917:   Elizabeth Murphy House built in Shorewood

1917:   A. B. Groves Building Co. House built in Madison

1919:   Wright designs eighteen concrete cottages in Racine, commissioned by Thomas P. Hardy, but never built

1921:   A. D. German Warehouse built in Richland Center

1922:   Divorces Kitty

1923:   Mother dies

1923:   Marries Maude "Miriam" Noel

1924:   Noel leaves Taliesin

1924:   Meets Olgivanna Lazovich Hinzenberg

1925:   Electrical fire destroys bungalow at Taliesin

1925:   Olgivanna moves to Taliesin

1925:   Daughter Iovanna born

1926:   Women's Building at Inter-County Fairgrounds demolished

1926:   Lake Mendota Boathouse demolished

1927:   Divorces Noel

1928:   Marries Olgivanna

1932:   Establishes Taliesin Fellowship with Olgivanna

1932:   Construction begins on the Hillside Drafting Studio

1933:   Former Taliesin gymnasium renovated into the Hillside Theatre and completed by Taliesin apprentices at Hillside Home School II

1934–35: Robert M. Lamp Cottage destroyed in fire

1937:   Herbert and Katherine Jacobs I House built in Madison

1938:   Wright appears on the cover of *Time* magazine

1938–39: Herbert F. Johnson House ("Wingspread") built in Wind Point

1938–41: Charles and Dorothy Manson House built in Wausau

1939:   SC Johnson Administration Building built in Racine

1940:   John C. Pew House built in Shorewood Hills

1940:   Bernard and Fern Schwartz House ("Still Bend") built in Two Rivers

1946:   Stepdaughter Svetlana dies with her young son in a car accident

1946–48: Herbert and Katherine Jacobs II House built in Middleton

1948:   Albert and Edith Adelman House built in Fox Point

1949–51: First Unitarian Society Meeting House built in Shorewood Hills

1950:   SC Johnson Research Tower built in Racine

1950:   Hillside Home School I demolished at Taliesin

1950:   Richard C. Smith House designed in Jefferson
1951–53: Patrick and Margaret Kinney House built in Lancaster
1952:   Hillside Home School II fire partially destroys building's southern wing
1954:   E. Clarke and Julia Arnold House built in Columbus
1955:   Granted an honorary doctorate of fine arts from the UW-Madison
1955:   Construction of Hillside Theater and Dining Room at Taliesin complete
1956:   Dr. Maurice Greenberg House built in Dousman
1956:   Eugene Van Tamelen House built in Madison
1957:   Willard Keland House built in Mount Pleasant
1957:   Arnold Jackson House built in Madison
1957:   Frank Iber House built in Plover
1957:   Wyoming Valley School built in Wyoming
1957–59: Walter Rudin House built in Madison
1958:   Seth Peterson Cottage built in Mirror Lake
1958:   Joseph Mollica House built in Bayside
1958:   Duey and Julia Wright House built in Wausau
1959–61: Annunciation Greek Orthodox Church built in Wauwatosa
1959:   Dies in Phoenix at the age of ninety-one, after intestinal surgery
1970:   The Geneva Inn/Lake Geneva Hotel demolished
1976:   Taliesin declared a National Historic Landmark
1985:   Arnold Jackson House relocated to Beaver Dam
1992:   Romeo and Juliet Windmill reconstructed at Taliesin
1993:   Taliesin acquires the Spring Green Restaurant and converts it to the Frank Lloyd Wright Visitor Center
1994:   Taliesin named by the National Trust for Historic Preservation as among the world's most endangered buildings
1994:   Frank Lloyd Wright Visitor Center in Spring Green opens for tours
1994:   Wright and Like tour launches in Madison, initially called Wright Here in Wisconsin
1997:   Monona Terrace Community and Convention Center built in Madison (based on Wright's 1938–1959 design)
2000:   Preservation of Taliesin's drafting studio complete
2010:   Olgivanna's restored bedroom at Taliesin opens to the public
2011:   Taliesin celebrates 100th anniversary and is removed from the National Trust for Historic Preservation's list of most endangered buildings
2015:   Preservation of Loggia at Taliesin completed and open to the public
2015:   Wisconsin and the world celebrate the 150th anniversary of the birth of Frank Lloyd Wright
2017:   Tan-Y-Deri House's interior and exterior restoration completed at Taliesin
2017:   Frank Lloyd Wright Trail created

Key Terms to Understanding Wright's Designs

American System-Built Homes (ASB Homes): Based on more than 900 drawings Wright made between 1912 and 1917, these homes for the working class were based on model designs, of which only about twenty were built, and twenty are still standing.

banquettes: This built-in seating along the length of a room—often in the living rooms of Wright's homes—features cushions for comfort and storage underneath.

built-in furnishings: So as not to disrupt a room's flow, and also allow for multipurpose uses, Wright's built-in furnishings included pullout chairs from a desk, built-in desks and dining tables, and multiple open shelving for books or decorative objects.

cantilever: A beam or truss projecting beyond its supporting wall. Wright exploited this structural principle in his work to create flat roofs and soaring terraces.

Cherokee Red: This favorite, beloved color of Wright's is akin to the shade of tomato soup, with an orange-red hue.

clerestory windows: These small windows appear in a row, band, or series above eye level and near the roofline.

compression and release: By entering into a cramped, tight space with a low ceiling, this created a grand entry just beyond with high, soaring ceilings and an open layout.

conspicuous entrances: Wright loved to surprise people, and that includes eschewing the common design of an American home where the front door often faced the street. Many of his homes feature a front door off to the side, or in an otherwise discreet location.

horizontal lines: Just like it sounds, an emphasis on building and designing outward instead of upward, as it relates to the roofline and window orientation.

organic architecture: This term, first coined by Wright, refers to when buildings are inspired by and literally built into their natural surroundings, with few disruptions to the landscape.

Prairie style: During the early 1900s, Wright and a few other architects designed homes in the Chicago area as an extension of the Arts and Crafts movement, embodying simplicity in their form, but craftsmanship at a deep level.

prefab: Much like the Montgomery Ward house kits where buyers had few choices and the materials were shipped with each order, Wright worked with two developers on prefab homes (Marshall Erdman and Arthur Richards).

radiant floor heating: Among the first architects to adopt this design, which hid "ugly" components of heating beneath the floor and kept owners' bare feet continually warm, Wright adopted this in nearly all of his homes after the 1937 Jacobs I House.

taproot design: Inspired by the growth of a plant or tree, Wright used this concept at the SC Johnson Research Tower in Racine.

textile block style: Linked to Wright's Mayan Revival period during the early 1920s, the concrete-block design of repeated patterns is seen in the A. D. German Warehouse in

Richland Center and several Southern California homes, including the Ennis House and Millard House ("La Miniatura").

Usonian Automatic: Designed in the early 1950s, this offshoot from Wright's Usonian designs was built from concrete blocks and resulted in seven homes, including the Benjamin Adelman House in Phoenix (1952).

Usonian style: As an affordable, design-rich house, these lacked basements, attics, and frills; the first was in 1937 (Jacobs House I).

Albert and Edith Adelman House, Fox Point
Tour info: This is a private residence and not open for tours. Please respect the owners' privacy.

It's rare to come across a Wright house that has been in the same family since its construction. That's the case with the Albert Adelman, a Usonian-style home in this northern Milwaukee suburb a few blocks west of the Lake Michigan shoreline. The 3,000-square-foot home was built in 1948 for Albert and Edith Adelman on a 2.5-acre lot. Albert was the son of Benjamin Adelman, who later commissioned a Wright home in Phoenix, in 1952.

Craig Adelman, chairman and founder of Adelman Travel Group, currently resides in the house and can easily recall childhood memories growing up here. He even remembers meeting Wright, although he was too young to converse with him on the same level as his parents. When I toured the home and met with Craig and his son, Jono, to write a story about the Adelman House for *Milwaukee Magazine* in 2017, the elder Adelman described Wright as a persistent visitor to the home who always wore a tall hat and donned a cape—and skillfully asked his parents for more money. He also remembers Wright demanding that the family replace forty birch-veneer doors with cypress—simply to honor his design, not their wants or desires.

In 1948, Wright was rising into favor—helped by the Fallingwater design completed in 1937—and busy working on drawings for the Guggenheim Museum in New York City. It's likely his apprentices were tasked with following through on his residential commissions, maybe even making decisions more theirs and not his.

In 2011, Adelman hired The Kubala Washatko Architects—their other projects include the First Unitarian Society Meeting House in Madison's addition—on designing and building a 700-square-foot pool house and an in-ground pool. The patio was also enlarged. This

project was the first major restoration of the home since it was constructed. Only the pool was in the original design. Due to budget constraints, it was never built.

In the pool house is an indoor kitchen and bar, as well as ample storage for hanging towels and clothing, and changing rooms, built-in lockers, a shower room, and a bath. There is also an outdoor lanai.

This design achieves similar geometry. For example, the pool house maintains a consistent eave height with the residence, but incorporates a flat roof and old cypress-wood siding in contrast to the hip roof and buff-colored concrete block exterior of the residence.

Throughout this process, the goal with the home, says Washatko, was to "restore it back to its historical character." The house was also built for 1940s living—not for today. "It wasn't very energy-efficient," he says. "Back then if you got cold you just turned the heat up." New heating and cooling units now do the trick, and four are concealed: for example, one's behind a built-in bench, and another's hidden in a closet.

Other work at that time included ripping out the home's original red-stained radiant concrete floor, which had suffered from uneven settlement due to freezing conditions. "Imagine

taking the entire concrete floor out of that house," says Washatko. Each tile had to be inventoried in order to return them to their rightful, original places. The copper radiant floor heating system was swapped out for a modern version, installed over a new gravel base and insulation. New concrete flooring was poured with red topping to match the original specifications. All exterior and interior concrete-block walls were stripped of lime wash, paint, and grime, then repaired or replaced with color-matching new material. Cypress board-and-batten walls were stripped and selectively restained to unify the wood color.

To better suit modern-day cooking needs, the kitchen was also updated. A new, expanded primary bath features a soaking tub and walk-in shower, along with recessed lighting, a wall of built-in storage, and concrete flooring stained red. There's a clear symmetry throughout this home as you flow from room to room.

Inside, the home boasts brick walls with cypress finishes, and—like many Wright Usonians—a fireplace and built-in shelves in the living room. Indirect lighting guides one down the hallway while also casting a warm, cozy glow, as I wrote in the *Milwaukee Magazine* article. The home features five bedrooms.

Annunciation Greek Orthodox Church, Wauwatosa
Tour info: Tours for groups (prices for groups up to 15 people or less than 15 people), or visit during the Divine Liturgy Sundays at 9 a.m. annunciationwi.org

There comes a time in every church's history where a new building is needed. The facilities no longer suit congregants' needs, or maybe the membership has outgrown the space.

In 1952, the Annunciation Greek Orthodox Church was in this exact spot. A thirty-eight-member building committee was quickly formed to find a new site—the small building in downtown Milwaukee wasn't going to do it anymore—and find an architect to come up with a design.

On a tour of the church's interior, you can see it's divided into three sections—the narthex, the nave, and the sanctuary. An example of poured-concrete construction, the church is crowned by a 104-foot-diameter dome and gold cross, which symbolizes Christ's unity of heaven and earth. This is also a familiar icon in Byzantine architecture.

Even in the beginning stages, no one in the church—not even the building committee—could have anticipated that this would be a process taking many years, and that Wright would be designing their church. In the end, this new church represented many things. First, that the local Greek-immigrant population had "made it" in terms of success, stature, and money, but also, that the church was thriving. This congregation, founded in 1906, was among the first ten Greek Orthodox parishes in the United States. Wright himself dubbed it his "little jewel" to Hagia Sophia, and also "St. Sophia," a nod to the seat of the Byzantine Empire in what was known as Constantinople, now Istanbul, Turkey.

On a tour of the saucer-shaped design one morning, tour guide and parishioner Catherine Spyres tells the story about her father, who, as a member of the building committee, had a heavy hand in writing this church's history.

Her father, Christ Seraphim, known in the community as Honorable Christ T. Seraphim, a circuit judge for Milwaukee County, sat on the building committee. After the committee had interviewed possible architects to hire and whittled the selections down to the finalists, he spoke up. According to both Spyres and accounts in John Gurda's *New World Odyssey: Annunciation Greek Orthodox Church and Frank Lloyd Wright*, Seraphim asked if anyone had interviewed Wright. His reasons were solid. How could he decide who was the best architect if Wright hadn't been considered?

Committee members' reactions were mixed. Some thought he was dead. Others couldn't imagine he'd be interested in designing their little church. Didn't he have more prominent commissions to handle? Still others viewed Wright as a subject of controversy—both for his off-the-wall designs and his known extramarital affairs. Not to mention the fact that he was quite expensive and always over budget. Seraphim held his ground. He refused to vote until Wright was contacted about any interest he might have in building their new church.

Faced with a budget, the committee forged on. They had developed a plan to raise additional money for their 700-seat church by asking each household to submit a $300 pledge. With 829 households, this promised to be effective. Their budget was further bolstered with $50,000 already in the bank. In the end, the church cost around $1.5 million. The church was forced to take out a $350,000 loan.

At the meeting, Wright placed a saucer upside down on top of his coffee cup and told the building committee that this was their design. While at first they were shocked, he went on to explain. It helped that Wright's third wife, Olgivanna, had been raised Serbian Orthodox. He surprisingly knew quite a bit about Byzantine design. Spyres remembers her dad telling her the coffee-cup story later. "Everyone's eyes were like, 'What did we do?' Once they calmed down, they agreed," she says.

The church lost its original building site when Milwaukee County announced plans to build an expressway through it—which was never built. But the eventual site, on the northwest corner of Milwaukee adjacent to the Wauwatosa border, ended up being perfect. And there was clearly enough land on which to build.

They broke ground on May 17, 1959, five weeks after Wright's death. On July 2, 1961, the church was officially dedicated. "It's a blend of what Frank Lloyd Wright did for us with his design, but it's based on our faith—Orthodox Christianity," says Spyres. It's important to note that the current windows, installed during the 1980s, were not designed by Wright.

The low ceiling in the entry of the church represents a place of contemplation before entering. This is not unlike Wright's commitment to using "compression and release" in many of his other buildings, where the ceiling height opens up in the main space, whether it's a sanctuary or a living room. The set of double doors leading past the entry bears its own story, representing the family tree of Jesus. He also incorporated, in the nave (the center of the church), the sign of the cross in a circle that's nearly hidden, but there. During services, the sanctuary is separated from the nave behind an iron screen that faces east.

Blue and gold are the dominant interior colors to represent colors of the ancient Byzantine Empire. A dozen rows of seating represent the twelve apostles, and the three sections represent Father, Son, and Holy Spirit. There are four vents for the sign of the cross. Another intentional choice was for each spire: The twelve bulbs are for each of the apostles. A recurring motif in the church's interior is a circle with a Byzantine cross and equilateral sides. Gold carpeting on the altar was replaced with granite in later years.

Spyres recalls when it was first built. "There was nothing out here in the 1950s. People who lived in the neighborhood said, 'What, that flying saucer?' Being built by Frank Lloyd Wright really put our church on the map," she says. Like other Wright designs, function overcame beauty. His plan to install 2-by-2-inch shiny ceramic tiles on the domed roof worked great—until they started popping off. The church painted the top of the dome blue instead. In 1980 a cross was added on top, not part of the original design.

September 12, 1971, is a date Spyres recalls vividly. It was the church's planned consecration and also the spontaneous baptism of William Wesley Peters and Svetlana Alliluyeva's baby girl, Olga. Peters had been Wright's head draftsman and protégé, and also the widowed husband to Wright's stepdaughter, Svetlana Hinzenberg Wright. As for Alliluyeva, she was Soviet leader Joseph Stalin's daughter. Later, she adopted the name Lana Peters to further distance herself from her family.

"This church was packed. On that day, Wesley asked to have his daughter baptized and asked my parents to be godparents. My mom, sister, and I went to Marshall Field's to get booties and other items," she says. Svetlana stayed behind at the church. "We found out later, with Svetlana being here, the KGB was in the parking lot." The two women were told not to run to their cars, so as to arouse suspicion, and to calmly head out to buy the necessary items and then quickly return. After this celebratory day, the two families remained in touch, including swimming outings and hosting visits at Spyres's childhood home.

In 1974 the church was listed on the National Register of Historic Places.

Although guided tours are for groups of a minimum of fifteen people, the church is open to the public during Doors Open Milwaukee, the third weekend in September each year. Another option for visiting is during either a Sunday service or the church's "Taste of Greece" event in late February. "We've had Frank Lloyd Wright people from all over the world [tour the church, including] from Taiwan and Australia," says Spyres.

Arthur R. Munkwitz Duplex Apartments, Milwaukee
Tour info: This building is no longer standing, as a result of a boulevard-widening project in 1973.

In what is now a neighborhood just west of Marquette University, and home to many of its off-campus students, there once existed an apartment building designed by Wright.

The project was born out of connections Wright had made with builders and developers while designing the American System-Built Homes, a process that resulted in more than 900 drawings. Only about twenty are still standing today.

What these all had in common were a desire to appeal to the working-class population with high-design concepts built using mass-production methods.

In 1916, the Arthur R. Munkwitz Duplex Apartments debuted at 1102–1112 N. 27th Street. There were four units in each of the two buildings. With pebble-dash stucco exteriors, they were part of the American System-Built Homes portfolio; more specifically, model J521, one of the 128 models developed between 1912 and 1916, based on more than 900 of Wright's drawings. As William Allin Storrer describes in his book, *The Architecture of Frank Lloyd Wright: A Complete Catalog*, each unit contained a living room that spanned the width, an adjoining dining space overlooking the entry, and a kitchen in the front, with two bedrooms and a bath in the rear.

Then, in 1973, they were torn down.

"They were demolished because [the city] wanted to widen Highland Boulevard into a boulevard," says Nicholas Hayes, author of *Frank Lloyd Wright's Forgotten House: How an Omission Transformed the Architect's Legacy*, and an expert on American System-Built Homes. "They were [also] in disrepair." Wright's or the developer Arthur Richards's choice to select pebble-dash stucco might have sealed their fate. "It was a questionable exterior treatment in Wisconsin winter," says Hayes. "You can imagine in the '70s if [the owner] was looking at it,

'How are we going to cover it with something different?' this would have cost a lot of money to recover."

An entrepreneur, Munkwitz was the president of the American Realty Service Company and Richards its vice president, says Hayes. The ideology behind the American System-Built Homes—to build as many homes as possible and earn a limitless profit—didn't jibe with Wright's ethos. "They were built for someone else to make money on," says Hayes. "That was one of the things that drove Wright away. The real-estate people were all making money, which was different than [building] these as affordable homes. Dabbling in Wright's brand name was a way of making a profit."

Still, despite the apartments' short life span, they achieved publicity. "Richards and Munkwitz were pretty darn good at public relations, at writing their own press releases, and got a story in the *Milwaukee Journal* that talked about Wright's brilliance and the organic-design principle."

Hayes notes that what makes the American System-Built Homes, including these apartments, different from many of Wright's other residential commissions is the lack of a signature art-glass window design unique to each. The American System-Built portfolio featured only a limited number of art-glass window designs, "because they weren't [yet] going to be purchased," says Hayes. That's because of the showroom model for these types of homes, where buyers later picked out what they wanted. "He did those [windows] last, just before shipping off for construction," says Hayes. For the Munkwitz Apartments' windows, Wright chose a design with a five-sided chevron inside the leadwork.

Burnham Block, Milwaukee

Tour info: Guided tours are held Saturdays for an entry fee. Reservations are required. One of the houses (with three bedrooms) is available for overnight stays through VRBO.com. wrightinmilwaukee.org

When you consider all of Wright's jewels across the country, a true gem is this block-long example on Milwaukee's South Side of American System-Built Homes. From the street, the six homes—two one-story homes and four two-story homes—are striking with their level of craftsmanship, although the story of how these came to be is equally fascinating.

Add on to that the intense amount of preservation by a team of volunteers—formed in 1992 as a nonprofit, now called Frank Lloyd Wright's Burnham Block—and it's an even more remarkable tale. In 1985 the block earned a spot on the National Register of Historic Places as the Burnham Street District.

By 1915, Wright had designed homes that were unaffordable for much of America—including the Darwin D. Martin House in Buffalo (1902–1905) and the Avery Coonley House in Riverside, Illinois (1908–1912). He felt a desire to create homes better suited for a

wider audience. They would cost less to buy but still feature most of his trademark designs, although using mass-production methods to bring building and supply costs down.

"At this point in his career, [Wright had] designed 130 homes, mostly in the Midwest, and [for] wealthy clients," says Burnham Block curator Michael Lilek, who grew up a few blocks away. "How [could] he create and design homes for a wider audience?"

By partnering with a developer, Arthur Richards, Wright saw a way to make this dream come true. Richards had already contracted with Wright in designing a hotel in Lake Geneva, a project that would eventually be built in 1912, but face demolition in 1970. Assisting with the insane number of drawings that were needed to help sell the concept was draftsperson Russell Barr Williamson. According to an article in the Summer 2010 *Frank Lloyd Wright Quarterly*, published by the Frank Lloyd Wright Foundation, the arrangement was to go like this: Wright could become a stockholder and sit on the board of Richards's company, and while it was Richards's company, Wright could earn royalties on sales.

"This was Wright choosing a vehicle to take his designs across the country," says Lilek, "and it was written into the contract that they would also go into Canada, Mexico, and across the Atlantic. Richards can't do it without this world-class designer and Wright can't do it without Richards. Richards was the sales guy, the marketing guy, and the fulfillment guy."

Would-be buyers could select from about thirty models and learn more about the features through partner dealers across the country. Full-page ads were taken out in the *Chicago Tribune* and other newspapers advertising this new housing model, called American System-Built Homes. The title of the *Chicago Tribune* ad in July 1917 read, "You Can Own an American Home."

But despite more than 900 drawings Wright created for the American System-Built Homes between 1911 and 1917, few were built. Wright pulled the plug on the project, walking away after a dispute with Richards, and leaving him without the noted architect. "He spent more time on this than anything he worked on," says Lilek. Had Wright stuck with the project, would his career—and the impression of his body of work many decades later—have shifted in this way? We'll never know.

"He wanted you to have a quiet and serene space to come home to at the end of the day," says Lilek. These were adaptable in versions from Pacific Ready Cut and Montgomery Ward. Today there are about twenty known American System-Built Homes identified and still standing—less than the twenty to thirty originally built. Wisconsin is home to nine, including six as part of the Burnham Block, and one each in Madison, Shorewood, and Oshkosh. According to the Summer 2010 *Frank Lloyd Wright Quarterly* article, in August 1917 Wright launched proceedings to nullify the contract he'd signed with Richards and Williamson. On what grounds? Soon he was in Japan designing the Imperial Hotel's annex, an epic project that, like the American System-Built Homes, was met with tragedy. It survived the 1923 Great Kanto earthquake but was demolished in 1968, with the entrance lobby saved and reconstructed, and moved to a different site. Or had the economic and lifestyle effects of World War I also compromised the dream of affordable housing? Fewer people were buying homes, unsure of the country's future and that of their own pocketbooks. "I think the true demise of this [was] World War I," says Lilek.

As for the Burnham Block, Richards erected the six structures on a site he acquired in 1915, in the 2700 block of West Burnham Street. The process for completion was quick: Construction began that October and wrapped up by the following July, in 1916. Considering the profile of potential buyers, it was an ideal site because streetcar lines were three blocks away, and the new 27th Street viaduct (appealing to automobile owners) was also nearby, along with a rising number of Polish immigrants who resided on the South Side in what were referred to—and still are today—as "Polish flats." These were essentially two-family duplexes with separate entrances, the units stacked on top of one another. On some lots, an additional structure,

such as a small cottage, was also built. Many of the homes in the area were built with expensive materials and consisted of a larger footprint than what many could afford, notes Lilek, in an article he wrote about the block for Wright in Milwaukee. Still, this urban density seemed to demand better options than what currently existed.

Utilizing model names Richards and Wright developed, the structures are: Two-Family, Flat C (2732–2734 W. Burnham St.); Two-Family, Flat C (2728–2730 W. Burnham St.); Two-Family, Flat C (2724–2726 W. Burnham St.); Two-Family, Flat C (2722 W. Burnham St.); Model B1 (2714 W. Burnham St.); and Model C3 (1835 S. Layton Blvd.).

There was a rhyme and a reason for each model name. Each began with a letter representing the type of design, followed by numerals indicating variations on the design. Similar to how new-build homes work today, the buyer first picks out a model and then moves on to selections in the interior; for example, cabinetry and fixtures. Only there was one difference between modern-day developers and the system Richards and Wright set up: Furnishings could also be chosen. Wright had clear intentions for how to use these tiny homes, and having the appropriate furniture made a lot of sense. Many homeowners would have to discard their earlier furnishings if they were relocating from a larger space. It's also possible that mass-produced furnishings sold at retailers wouldn't fit into these homes. And even if they did, the synergy of Wright's furnishings within a Wright home couldn't be beat.

One example is the breakfast nook with Wright-designed benches and a table folded into the design. It wasn't a separately defined dining space like in most homes. But the open layout appealed to those who yearned for natural light, as a result of fewer walls and more windows, and a free-flowing space. Sleeping porches were also added to the duplexes, to help contend with concern around tuberculosis breakouts during this time. In Model C3, the building on the corner, there are two bedrooms, a living room, and built-ins serving as a "wall" between the living room and a wing to the bedrooms and bath. A covered porch provides additional space, particularly during the warmer months.

At 805 square feet, the Model B1, with its slate-gray exterior, is among the smallest of Wright's built designs for a single-family home. But what makes it feel roomier is the expansive terrace on the street side and the orientation of all windows, where light is always present during the daylight hours. In 2004, then-steward Norman Gabrielson sold it to Frank Lloyd Wright Wisconsin, which embarked on a thirteen-month restoration that included replacing original stucco on the exterior (due to asbestos and poor condition). Other tasks were to replace the concrete deck with a wood one. Then, on the interior, lost and damaged light fixtures and interior millwork were re-created, in an attempt to bring this house back to its original state.

"Every decision we make is [based on] 'What would the house look like on July 5, 1916?'" says Lilek, referring to the date of completion.

The first house to be restored was in 1981 when the Jillyane and David Arena bought one of the duplexes and spent three years renovating it. This work included creating eighty stained-glass windows that were designed for the home but never made. In 2011 they sold it to another family, who work with Frank Lloyd Wright's Burnham Block to lovingly maintain it, as well as rent it out for overnight stays. The nonprofit bought three other duplexes in 2005, 2007, and 2019. They are working to restore the building.

Just like the target buyers a little more than a century ago, the goal is to stock each of these homes with Wright-designed furnishings—including end tables, bedroom furniture, and an American System-Built Home upholstered barrel chair (never realized, and with more

slats than spindles than his other barrel-chair designs, plus an upholstered back)—for the full effect. A few artisans have already completed reproductions of these furnishings, and more are on their way.

This wasn't the only American System-Built Homes project in Milwaukee, but it's the only one still standing, unless you count the Elizabeth Murphy House in the near-north suburb of Shorewood. Just west of Marquette University, the Munkwitz Apartments (two quadplexes) were built in 1916, referred to as J521 in Wright's drawings—only to be razed in 1973 when the city wanted to widen Highland Boulevard. Why were they named Munkwitz? It all goes back to Richards's business dealings. Richards was vice president of American Realty Service Company, and Arthur R. Munkwitz, its president.

Today the Burnham Block is nearly flawless and hosts among the highest concentrations of Wright residential designs. One of the duplexes features an odd claim to fame for a Wright house: the only one in the world with aluminum siding. A few of the homes are open to the public during a guided tour, which helps provide revenue to fund ongoing restoration efforts. Visitors have arrived from thirty-seven countries and every US state, says Lilek. "On any given day, it's a constant stream of cars with people pulling up and taking pictures. We see just shy of five thousand visitors each year." Also, it's important to note, he says, that 60 percent of the people who tour one of the houses declare they could easily live in one, a testament to Wright's design decisions.

Elizabeth Murphy House, Shorewood
Tour info: This is a private residence and not open for tours. Please respect the owners' privacy. elizabethmurphyhouse.com

"You don't get to add any more books," says Nick Hayes, owner of this American System-Built Home just north of Milwaukee, as he gestures at the built-in shelves next to the fireplace. Indeed, one is featured proudly: *Walden* by Henry David Thoreau, fitting, as Hayes is an avid sailor and program director with the Milwaukee Community Sailing Center.

Including their book collection, Hayes and his wife Angela downsized their possessions before moving in, in 2016. But they couldn't be happier. Previously they lived in the same village—eight blocks away—but in a much larger house. The Elizabeth Murphy House, a Model A203, was completed in 1917 after two years of design work by Wright and his then-colleague Russell Barr Williamson, as draftsperson. Unlike other American System-Built Homes, which were a study in affordable housing, Arthur Richards was not the developer. Instead, he sold the drawings to Elizabeth Murphy, who hired contractor Herman F. Krause.

It's clear on a tour that every item in their home has its place. This is out of necessity. There is only so much storage, and only so much square footage (960 square feet). Hayes's home office—not included in the square footage—is on the now-closed-in sleeping porch, with cypress flooring and pebble-dash walls, a common feature in maritime climates such as Scotland, Wales, and the United Kingdom, as well as many American System-Built Homes. Five 21-inch-wide vertical windows flaunt original leaded glass. While there are just two bedrooms, both flood with natural light when it's sunny outside.

"This, to me, is the most amazing part," says Hayes, as he gestures this author to enter from the porch. A three-quarters wall to the left hides the living room. The low ceiling forces you to enter the social space's open layout, to immediately rid any feelings of being cramped or crowded in the entry. This is Wright's signature "compression and release."

The home's condition is immaculate, with original woodwork having never been painted over and the floors recently refinished by the Hayes family. An original built-in in the dining room features original cabinetry and knobs. Living-room shelves and some of the kitchen cabinets are also original. But it wasn't until Barbara Elsner, owner of the Frederick C. Bogk House on Milwaukee's East Side, toured the home during a Wright and Like tour that the dining room became complete.

"She [told Hayes], 'You've got it all wrong. You need to look at the drawings.'" In those drawings he learned that the table was to be pushed against the built-in, to provide greater flow. And, the original ceiling lighting was now synchronized to the table's new layout by being directly above.

Increasing flow became important to the Hayeses as they strove to remodel the kitchen for modern use while still honoring its historic roots. Back then, plug-in refrigerators weren't a thing, which meant the tall, awkwardly sized boxes did not clutter up the kitchen. Instead, an icebox kept items cold in the adjacent hallway.

Stainless-steel drawers beneath an espresso machine keep food items frozen or refrigerated. "We got the sight line back," says Hayes. They also swapped out the Formica countertops for birch. As for the lone bath, the fact that the floor sagged and had flooded was

a major deterrent to other potential buyers. But the Hayes family saw past it. They gutted and restored the bath, including adding radiant floor heating, and found a period-specific tub on Craigslist, one with the roller only an hour away in Sheboygan. The sink was sourced from New York.

"We've removed most of the inappropriate layers and restored the home to Wright's drawings, instructions, and spirit where modern codes allow," says Hayes.

After moving in, Hayes became obsessed—in a good way—with the house's origin, particularly because it had only been discovered to be a Wright-designed home the year prior. In 2021, he published a book about his findings, *Frank Lloyd Wright's Forgotten House: How an Omission Transformed the Architect's Legacy*, with the University of Wisconsin Press. He's also an expert on American System-Built Homes, of which there are about twenty (known and identified) still standing, despite more than 900 drawings created between 1911 and 1917. Between twenty and thirty of these homes were built before Wright walked away from the project, disillusioned and no longer enamored. In addition to the Elizabeth Murphy House, eight more are in Wisconsin, including six as part of the Burnham Block, one in Oshkosh (the Stephen M. B. Hunt II House), and one in Madison (the A. B. Groves Building Co. House).

"[Wright's] trying to be empathetic to the working class for the first time in his career," says Hayes. Whereas his previous commissions were only for the wealthy, these were designed for everybody else, and in partnership with Arthur Richards, a developer, along with draftsperson Russell Barr Williamson.

One of the reasons this home was only discovered to be a Wright design in 2015 is because of the rift between Wright and Richards, and the realization that the American System-Built Homes were now dead. Wright rarely, if ever, spoke of the affordable-housing concept again. "He omitted these homes from his vocabulary," Hayes says, about both Wright's and Richards's attitudes toward the Elizabeth Murphy House. That Williamson did not save any records also led to the home's provenance being lost. The 1976 addition of a garage began to quash any theories that this was a Wright house, because everyone knew he despised the look of garages and actually preferred carports. It would take a lot of visits to the house from a variety of Wright experts (including Traci Schnell and Richard Johnson), their research, and a report written by Michael Lilek, curator of the Burnham Block, to determine that, yes, indeed, this was a Wright home.

When the Elizabeth Murphy House was built, it was one of only a half-dozen homes on this block, which is now lined with houses that are close together and feature small, urban-sized yards. Across the street is a 1921 Russell Barr Williamson house. Hayes estimates there are at least seventeen similar homes in Shorewood designed by Williamson.

Frederick C. Bogk House, Milwaukee
Tour info: This is a private residence and not open for tours. Please respect the owners' privacy.

The first impression from the street of this nearly 9,000-square-foot home is that it's very stately. The entire façade is brick. As the only single-family home Wright designed in Milwaukee, it was built in 1917, three years after the murder of his mistress, Mamah Borthwick, and her children in a fire set by a servant at Taliesin.

Could it be that Wright dove into this project with his heart and soul as he grieved this recent loss? At the time, he was also ruminating over the ruin of Taliesin's residential wing after the fire and trying to redeem his career with drawings commissioned for two buildings at the Imperial Hotel in Tokyo. He did get the commission, only to have the annex survive the 1923 Great Kanto earthquake, and later demolished in 1968.

Although Wright's personal life and notable projects were in crumbles, he desperately wanted to shine again as an architect.

Like the Imperial Hotel, the Bogk House is a boxy design and features custom tile and a green, low-pitched hip roof. "What he basically did is turn the house into nature," says homeowner Margaret Howland, with the discreet entrance to the north one's first clue. The home has been on the National Register of Historic Places since 1972.

Inside, one walks up four steps and through a low-ceilinged hallway to the living room. Built-in banquettes surround the fireplace, which soars to the ceiling. Up another half-flight of stairs, in the back of the living room, is the dining room. There's another nod to bridging with nature, with walls of narrow leaded-glass windows inviting natural light and the surrounding greenery indoors. "To me, it's like a screen to the city," says Howland. A celadon-green ceiling in the living room is another nod to nature.

This is among Wright's first homes employing an open layout, moving away from the Victorian era of the late 1800s and early 1900s, where rooms were small and the ceilings high. This open layout is later seen in his Usonian-style homes.

But this is also a family home, and where Howland lives, as the second generation of her family to live in the home. Her parents, Robert and Barbara Elsner, purchased the home in 1955 and Barbara continues to live nearby. Changes they've made include repairing the roof with specially made replacement tiles and renovating the primary bath, as well as updating the kitchen, minus the original marble countertops and a stove dating back to the 1950s. There's an intentional effort to honor the period of the home while simultaneously bringing it up to modern standards.

"Everything that was designed for the home is now in the home," she says, the result of furnishings that either never left or were acquired from the Bogks' daughter. Built-in bookshelves and desks are in abundance, including a desk that juts out just before the fireplace appears. The ottomans are also part of Wright's original furnishings, although not designed for this home. The beautiful dining-room set, two chairs, and a side table were bought back from the Bogks' daughter by Howland's parents. "My parents just kept writing [to] her over and over until she sold," she says.

A palette of lime-green, tangerine-orange, mustard-yellow, and turquoise marks the living room's upholstered banquettes, and most furnishings and throw pillows. The rug is a copy of the original and based on what Wright designed for the home. It was installed during the 1960s. The original rug rests in the permanent collection at the Figge Art Museum in Davenport, Iowa, along with the Bogk House drawings. A water feature, while not currently operating, is a surprising yet relaxing amenity on the eyes. Above the dining-room built-in is a Chinese silk painting by Tang Yin, sourced by Wright.

Growing up in a Wright-designed home has furthered Howland's appreciation for his work. While as a teenager she yearned to rearrange her bedroom's furnishings—as all teens do—she found it impossible. Wright's anticipated use of the room was not flexible enough. "There's somewhat of a very controlling element to the house," she says. She even went to see what's left of the Imperial Hotel in Tokyo. "I had been traveling for three weeks alone. I had tea. I was like, 'Oh, I'm at home,'" she recalls.

On a family visit to Taliesin during the years when Wright and Olgivanna were running the fellowship, Howland was in awe. They were there on a Saturday evening for a function. "I felt like I was among royalty. [Olgivanna] sat like a queen. She sat there, straight. She was definitely in charge," she says. All the girls and women had long skirts on except for Howland and her sister. They were headed to a supper club for dinner after.

The home was built for Frederick C. Bogk, who lived there for several years. Bogk served as an alderman and also secretary-treasurer of the Ricketson Paint Works. He later added a powder room—within a former coat closet—says Howland. Mrs. Bogk had long admired the Avery Coonley House in Riverside, Illinois, and aspired to live in a house just like it. Indeed, there are remarkable similarities between the two homes, as noted in documents accompanying the 2013 *Frank Lloyd Wright: The Bogk House Drawings* show at the Figge Art Museum. This includes the window designs, as well as fabrics and surfaces.

Over the years, this home has had three owners. "My mom and dad are not ready to sell," says Howland, who now owns the home, "[so] we can have family events here." Thinking back to the day her parents bought the house, moving from nearby Whitefish Bay, it was a contrast to their other home, in Kettle Moraine, Wisconsin, filled with eclectic 1950s decor.

"I love the architecture and I love living in the architecture. Look at this," she says, gesturing her arms wildly around her, "the way the sun comes in." Stories of Wright's Milwaukee connections easily came to the family upon moving in, including a neighbor who recalled that Wright sat in front of her at the opera once and refused to take off his hat. Another neighbor remembers Wright showing up at her family's house with Japanese prints as payment.

A family trip to New York City to see the Museum of Modern Art show (*Frank Lloyd Wright at 150: Unpacking the Archive*) in 2017, timed with what would have been Frank Lloyd Wright's 150th birthday, reconfirmed that the decision to buy the house had been the right one. "She has a super good eye," says Howland about her mother. "She just walked in and it was like, 'This is it.'"

Dr. Maurice Greenberg House, Dousman

Tour info: This is a private residence and not open for tours. Please respect the owners' privacy.

Dave and Liz Riedel bought this Wright-designed, 3,000-square-foot Usonian home in 2005 after Liz read about the home in the local newspaper. They were already living nearby. The property was being divided with the intention of selling both parcels. Dave attended a zoning meeting and approached their agent.

"We were looking for a Midcentury Modern house for six years. I like to think of it as a reverse Usonian," says Dave. That's because it's not on flat land, like Wright's other Usonian designs. Instead, it's built into the hillside. "Entering the living room from the [home's] entrance feels like going into a theatre with the trees being the stage," says Dave. In the entry, Norman bricks were used—not limestone, like in Wright's plans. "The story goes that Maurice said to Wright, 'I can't afford it. The price is too high for limestone,'" says Dave. Wright suggested this long brick style instead.

A Wright-designed dining table and ottomans are in the open layout, where the dining and living areas are. Heading down the hallway to the south, there are three bedrooms and a bath. Within the footprint of their daughter's room is where the addition began. "This is where the old house ends and the new house begins," says Dave.

The home needed some updates and also a workshop for the couple's business, Riedel Electronics, which began with rebooting vintage Predicta TVs with modern parts so that viewers can tune into their favorite shows while appreciating a vintage lifestyle. It's since expanded into electrical engineering and repair of machine tools.

But the bigger job came next. Architect John Eifler—a seasoned restorer of Wright homes, including the Jacobs I house in Madison and the Dorothy and Charles Manson House in

Wausau—was tapped to build a wing based on Wright's designs that had never been completed. In the wing is a second bath along with three bedrooms, and a patio and reflecting pond, plus two replica Wright stone statues, like the ones at SC Johnson.

Still, two restorations had already taken place: in the 1970s and the 1980s. 1976, and in the late 1980s.

Eifler's work easily increased the amount of space for this family of three (their daughter is now off at college; and Dave's father has since moved in). The connections to Wright's original design in this new wing, which continues to be under construction, are nearly seamless, such as their daughter's built-in desk and cabinetry in a clear Usonian vein, featuring honey-stained wood. Eifler also gave Liz sage advice during the lengthy process of bringing this Wright home to its full potential, telling her, "'Remember, Liz, this is your house, not a museum.'"

The Riedels are only the second owners. They've quickly infused the interior with their collection of Midcentury Modern decorative arts and furnishings, including intricate wood carvings by Dave's great-grandfather, who emigrated from Slovenia in 1907. These are on display in a nook with a built-in banquette below. In the dining room, the couple's ceramic Tiki barware lines built-in horizontal shelves above the Danish-style dining table set. The family even owns and drives a 1961 Plymouth wagon in a cool icy-blue hue, which they bought in 1999.

Still, the restoration work is endless—and a labor of love. "The job for me is that I get it into a place that whenever it does leave our hands, it has been properly done," says Dave. "The reason I like architecture is because it combines creativity with reality. Everything you're doing, you're challenging the eye."

The home was built between 1954 and 1956 for Dr. Maurice Greenberg and his wife, Margaret. For reasons unknown, but suspected to be due to lack of funds, he never completed

the home's second wing. When the Riedels moved in, there was just one wing. Greenberg's office had evolved into a bedroom for the Greenbergs; since their adult son never lived at home, the one-bedroom, one-bath home was sufficient for their needs.

By consulting Wright's blueprints, as well as Greenberg's receipts for home repairs and utility expenses, the couple has been able to get the home back to what it should have been. It's also an intuitive process: "I take my cues off the house," Dave says. "Blueprints aren't bibles. They're guidelines. It's a work of art and we're the artists. We could be the only people in a position to complete Wright's design. How does that not fall into our laps, two miles from where we lived?"

Joseph Mollica House, Bayside

Tour info: This is a private residence and not open for tours. Please respect the owners' privacy.

As a commission for a local builder who specialized in Midcentury Modern homes, this prefab house in the North Shore community of Bayside remains solid and minimally retouched many decades later. Unfortunately, Wright never got to see this prefab house after it was completed in 1959. He died earlier that year.

Partnering with developer Marshall Erdman, Wright debuted three prefab designs (#1, #2, and #3). The Joseph Mollica House is a Prefab #1, flaunting an L-shape design with an open layout for the dining room, living room, and kitchen, centered around a nearly wall-length fireplace. At the Joseph Mollica House, the fireplace and some exterior walls were crafted from Lannon stone, sourced from the nearby village of Lannon. Other Prefab #1 designs in Wisconsin are the Arnold Jackson House in Beaver Dam, the Eugene van Tamelen House in Madison, and the Frank Iber House in Plover. A Prefab #2 example of Wright's design is the Walter Rudin House in Madison. None of the Prefab #3 designs were ever built.

By the time the 4,000-square-foot Joseph Mollica House was built, Wright and Erdman had already worked together on the First Unitarian Society Meeting House in Madison, as well as the Wyoming Valley School near Taliesin.

Tucked into a sloping bluff with a ravine in the backyard, this two-level beauty (main level and a walk-out lower level) features five bedrooms—four upstairs and one downstairs. It was enough to entice a couple, Sylvia Ashton and Nicholas Goodhue, to relocate from sunny Los Angeles.

Ashton grew up in Shorewood and Brookfield, but relocated with her family to Fresno, California, later working in San Francisco and Los Angeles. After returning to Wisconsin for a Ripon College reunion, she fell back in love with her home state.

"I was getting *Milwaukee Magazine* as some way to see what was going on [back home]," says Ashton. A Coldwell Banker ad for nine different homes caught her eye.

"One house sucked me in like a magnet, and it said 'Designed by Frank Lloyd Wright.' I couldn't believe it," she says, adding that in the photo, the house "was [surrounded by] snow. I couldn't tell what was the front [or the] back." It was this intriguing design that made the couple fly out to take a look.

They fell in love with the view from the foyer—how you could easily see into the backyard's mature trees, thanks to a wall of glass doors in the living room. In fact, if the wind is blowing just right, one can even hear the trees rustling.

By the time they'd moved in, in 2007, both knew about Wright's legacy and career. Ashton's cousin, an architectural draftsman, got her interested in Wright when she was a teenager. Indeed, Ashton once shared a dream with her mother. "I wanted to live in a Wright house. She said, 'Sylvia, that's not going to happen.' What a shock [when it did]!"

Goodhue's grandfather (Bertram Goodhue) was an architect who designed the Nebraska state capitol. This project was significant, because it's the first capitol building lacking a dome; instead, there's a tower that's central to the design. Nicholas's father was an architect, too, and worked on projects that include the Getty Villa in Malibu, California.

The couple served as docents when their home was on the Wright and Like tour (2011 and 2017) and the Frank Lloyd Wright Building Conservancy Tour (2015).

While the exterior was once a pastel green, it's now a warm cocoa color. Entering the home, the foyer leads to a sunken-style living room. Philippine mahogany plywood is wrapped around the home's interior, including walls and built-ins. The walk-out lower level features a second fireplace in the main room, along with built-in seating and open shelving. Down a hallway is a wet bar, walk-in closet, bath, and bedroom, all updated after Wright's original design. Fun story: Stone flooring in the downstairs bath and fireplace hearth was sourced from another Wright-designed home that shared the same restoration architect.

In two of the baths, the floor and wall tiles have not been altered since the home's construction, showcasing Wright's affinity for mauve, cream, black, and turquoise in a repeated pattern. At least two of the sinks are original, in almond and petal-pink. A Talk-A-Phone intercom system in the primary bedroom wasn't ever wired, but could be, as a new take on the smart-home concept. The previous owner's Arts and Crafts style wallpaper is the perfect fit in the family room and adjoining kitchen. There are eighty windows and eight outside entrances.

Other than a 1991 remodel of the lower level, and rebuilding the chimney shortly after this couple moved in, this home has remained intact, a testament to its sturdy design. The chimney work is also proof that Wright stewards share resources: Frederick C. Bogk House's Barbara Elsner recommended her mason.

But what sets this one apart, in the world of Wright homes and also his prefab designs, is the garage. It's perfect for chilly Wisconsin winters. Only four of the nine #1 prefab homes have garages.

RACINE

SC Johnson Administration Building and Research Tower, Racine

Tour info: All five tours of the SC Johnson campus are free with advance reservations, twice daily Wednesday–Sunday: Full SC Johnson Campus (90 minutes), SC Johnson Campus with Waxbird Commons (2 hours), Junior Architect Adventure Tour (90 minutes, designed for children), Wright Tour (90 minutes) and Wright at Night Tour (90 minutes). reservations.scjohnson.com

In 1936, H. F. Johnson Jr.—then the third generation of his family to serve as president of the cleaning-products company—recruited Wright to design a new building where the company had long been headquartered. Born in 1899, Johnson Jr. took over the company when his father died in 1928. He was only twenty-nine years old. The project took place in two phases: first, the Administration Building (1939), and later, the Research Tower (1950). Even if you never knew anything about Wright's designs, the looming fifteen-story tower with its Cherokee Red brick banding and Pyrex-glass tubes in the windows would catch your eye as you walked or drove through this largely residential neighborhood 1.5 miles south of downtown

Racine. A concrete core runs up the building's interior, noticeable with just the right amount of light shining through the building's many windows. It's a fine example of Wright's taproot design, taking its inspiration from plant and tree growth.

"He had a huge vision for what he wanted this to be," says Trout Rrowul, SC Johnson's archivist, about both the Administration Building and the Research Tower.

Much of this has proven to be timeless. On June 1, 2022, Steelcase announced the rerelease of furniture (desk, chair, and accessories) it initially produced—based on Wright's designs—for the SC Johnson Administration Building's Great Workroom, called The Frank Lloyd Wright Racine Collection by Steelcase. In 1985 Steelcase bought and restored the Wright-designed, Prairie-style Meyer May House in Grand Rapids, Michigan, not far from its company headquarters, as a thank-you for Wright giving them the furniture commission. The pieces honor Wright's original design, such as the two-tier, oval-shaped desktop; three swinging drawers off to the right; and the oval-shaped chair back. Another futuristic part of Wright's design for the Great Workroom was that it had air-conditioning—not very common in 1939.

Secretaries working in the Great Workroom reportedly gave tours to people who randomly stopped by. They were often enamored, as visitors are today, with the interior dendriform columns that are 18 feet tall at the top and 9.5 inches at the bottom. These almost weren't built, as the state denied their construction, feeling they could not support the roof. Wright disagreed, and, in a demonstration, piled 60 tons of iron and sandbags—five times the required load—on top to prove his point. The design sailed through. Only it wasn't a smooth trip from there. Like many Wright roofs, this one leaked, and employees knew to expect it with each storm. Janitors also knew to put out buckets whenever rain was in the forecast. In 2010, Pyrex-glass tubes used for lighting, and in the original design, were replaced with plastic versions. The glass tubes simply leaked too much when it rained.

Speaking of the female secretaries, their experience using the desks and chairs that Wright designed wasn't always pretty. These were part of a collection of forty furnishing types Wright designed for this space. Wright made them with three wheels, which is all well and good until you need to lean over to pick up a dropped pen, pencil, or other object. The fact that women were likely seated, with their legs crossed, meant they toppled over onto the floor. Johnson Jr. registered this complaint with Wright, but he didn't budge. Johnson Jr. set up a situation where Wright was seated in one of the chairs and a pencil slowly rolled off the edge of the desk. You can guess what happened next. Wright fell, which led to him revisiting the design so each chair now had four wheels, for better balance (and, one might argue, improved safety).

Another feature of the Great Workroom that needed to be amended was the red-rubber flooring chosen by Wright. It became costly to maintain with damage caused by women's high-heeled shoes.

According to Mark Hertzberg's *Frank Lloyd Wright's SC Johnson Research Tower*, Johnson first pitched the idea to Wright to "build up" and not out, but Wright had already been working on concepts for towers. Johnson may have asked, "Why not go up in the air?" but Wright was already tinkering with tower designs. Price Tower in Bartlesville, Oklahoma, wasn't yet built (that came in 1956), but in 1927–1929, Wright created drawings for a group of twenty-story apartment buildings in New York City called St.-Mark's-in-the-Bouwerie. They were

never realized, but teased Wright with the idea of building a taproot tower one day. Hertzberg also writes in his book that in 1924, Wright designed a proposal for the National Life Insurance Company in Chicago that included a tower.

Like the Joh Martin ... the Renamed building, each floor of the Research Tower is actually two stories, providing the appearance of more room than there actually is, due to the high ceilings. In the open space, each ceiling soared to 18 feet. Another way Wright borrowed from his other designs was with the advertising department's glass-dome ceiling in the Administration Building. This was a skylight design he created for the Guggenheim Museum in 1943.

What Wright and Johnson Jr. disagreed on regarding the Administration Building was location. Being the organic architect that he was, Wright wanted it to be built 10 miles west of the current site, nestled in nature, with shops and homes for the employee to utilize and reside in. Johnson Jr. didn't go for it, and Wright went along with the original plan to build on the current site. "Wright turned the office building inward," explains Hertzberg, "and shielded the workers from the surrounding urban environment."

Wright almost didn't get the commission to build the Research Tower. According to Hertzberg, Johnson Jr. had concerns about repeating the Administration Building's "financial mess" and construction delays, which he wrote to Wright about in 1943. But Johnson Jr. also believed in symmetry. To have a tower like this would accent the campus's overall look. If only Johnson Jr. could have foreseen the future. The tower ended up costing $3.5 million, up from the $1.2 million updated cost in 1946, and much higher than what Wright had originally pitched, $750,000.

In November 1950 the Research Tower was finally dedicated. It closed during the early 1980s when the company's research and development team moved across the street. There were very valid, functional reasons for the relocation. First, the stairwell was only 30 inches

in width, and cited as a fire hazard by the local fire marshal, as this was the only exit. But more importantly, there was no room for expansion as the Tower was only designed for fifty chemists.

In 2014 tours of the Research Tower were offered for the first time, providing non-employees with a glimpse at this unique workplace design by Wright. On a tour, it's as if the laboratory is stuck in a 1950s time warp, with original furnishings crafted by Hamilton Manufacturing in Two Rivers, and other lab gadgets on display as much as possible, allowing visitors to see and experience what it looked like during the tower's debut. While the benches were once painted Wright's beloved Cherokee Red, and later painted over, it's easy to close your eyes and imagine a workspace here decades ago, as Wright intended.

You'll also note two stone statues in the courtyard. These 16-foot-tall statues were erected in 1979, but based on Wright's 1924 designs for a proposed clubhouse at the Nakoma Country Club near Madison. He had called them "Nakoma" and "Nakomis," as a tribute to male and female Native Americans in the Winnebago tribe, present in Southern Wisconsin and now referred to as the Ho-Chunk Nation. The country club was never realized. Wright apprentice William Wesley Peters designed two gates that are largely unchanged. They were added in 1968–1969.

Thomas P. Hardy House, Racine

Tour info: This is a private residence and not open for tours. Please respect the owners' privacy.

While many of Wright's house designs are mirrored within one another, this one near downtown Racine is completely unique.

For one, there are a deceiving number of levels inside—seven, to be exact, despite the house looking like two stories from the curb. And while with its hipped roof and stucco exterior, it's categorized as an example of Wright's Prairie-style designs, it is still a detour from any of his other projects.

The 2,200-square-foot house has had seven owners since it was built in 1905 for a local attorney (Thomas P. Hardy), and is currently owned by Thomas and Joan Szymczak. As Mark Hertzberg describes in his book, *Frank Lloyd Wright's Hardy House*, it was known as the "kooky" house because it looked completely different from the other European-revival-style homes on the street at that time. Could this have been an opportunity for Wright to express his distaste for those styles by designing something on the other end of the spectrum?

Hardy commissioned Wright to design the house in 1904. What was to be a happy family house ended up being anything but. By 1912, writes Hertzberg, Hardy was collecting rental income from the home, living elsewhere in Racine, perhaps occupied with his costly and contentious divorce and unsuccessful custody battle, rather than living in an architectural masterpiece.

In 1937 the house was sold in a sheriff's auction from the steps of the courthouse, effectively removing it from Hardy's ownership. The Sporer family purchased it for $6,500. Despite this change in stewards, Hardy kept fighting for control of the house, winning a court order later that year to retain ownership—if he could raise $5,500 in the next three months. In 1937 he even went so far as to beg H. F. Johnson Jr., then president of SC Johnson, for aid. But the Depression was crimping everyone's spending. Who would want to take this on during a financial crisis anyway? Hardy's last-ditch effort was a proposal to pay a $1,000 bonus to anyone who could supply the $5,500 loan. In the end, the Sporers got the house they wanted.

While, again, the design is completely unique, it does fall within Wright's portfolio, and he no doubt found inspiration from two sources. In 1893 he observed the Japanese pavilion at the World's Columbian Exposition, held in Chicago. Although the roof on one of the structures sloped further upward, the way it was smartly packaged and conceived in a boxy, geometric design bears organic-design principles, with surprises within. "There are [also] some similarities to the Frederick F. Tomek House in Riverside, [Illinois]," says Hertzberg, another example of Wright's Prairie designs.

With two front doors (tucked out of sight and, until the 1940s or 1950s, behind decorative wood gates), flanked by a courtyard on each side, the house is eye-catching. It's equally so once you step inside. The obvious compression and release technique of Wright's happens in the entry, where you stand in a narrow space with 6-and-a-half-foot ceilings, then proceed up six steps into the living room. One note of interest in this entryway is a bank of leaded-glass windows depicting the floor plan of the house. The entire east-facing wall of the living room,

and the dining room eight steps below that, looks out over Lake Michigan. In addition to the living room's two stories of windows, there's a fireplace stretching to the balcony and faced in Roman brick. Considering these are 17-foot ceilings, this is quite a feat. The kitchen, being partly below ground level, seems almost like an afterthought, when today, kitchens are the heart of the home.

From the living room, it's eleven steps to the balcony and bath, then two more to the upper-level bedrooms. Two bedrooms are also just off the living room.

Outdoor spaces are in abundance for use on a warm day, including a terrace off the dining room and the aforementioned courtyards. A new deck was added two years ago, and before that, after World War II, the downstairs level was further built out for post-beach fun, with a shower (to rinse off sand) and rec room (inviting friends over to play). In the two south-facing bedrooms are pullout chairs designed by Wright and artfully tucked into the built-in desks (also used as dressing tables). The dining room's chandelier is another nod to Wright, as it's a more recent reproduction of the one hanging in the Dana-Thomas House in Springfield, Illinois.

"Occasionally, when a car goes by, you see a shadow on that wall," says Hertzberg, as he gestures to the back wall of the entry hall, where the seven entry-hall windows' leaded-glass pattern casts a shadow. He knows the house like the back of his hand, as the subject of his research, but also having known its stewards.

Much of the restoration work occurred when Gene Szymczak—the brother and brother-in-law to Thomas and Joan Szymczak—acquired the property in 2012. He worked on it tirelessly until his 2016 death. While living in the house was a new experience for him, he knew its presence well. "Gene had a summer job with the city garbage removal [service] and picked up garbage in the [home's] courtyard," explains Hertzberg. "The house had struck a chord

with him." Through his work in writing the book, Hertzberg had gotten to know the previous owners, Margaret and Jim Yoghourtjian.

"Gene called me and said 'Is the Hardy House for sale?' Margaret and Jim gave me permission to take him through the house," recalls Hertzberg. "Gene looked at me and said, 'I have no children. This is something I can do for Racine.' I thought the Yoghourtjians and the Szymczaks should meet." Hertzberg advised Szymczak to bring Margaret's favorite pastry: chocolate marzipan from Larsen's Bakery. That extra touch sure helped. "Gene made them an offer for the house," he says, which was immediately accepted.

Anne Sporer Ruetz was a member of one of the families who lived in the Hardy House. As a young girl, she moved in with her parents, an aunt, and a cousin, living there until they moved out in 1947. "My mother had never been inside the house," she says, recalling how her father came home one day and announced he'd bought a house. "Can you imagine that?" But she knew it well, having lived two doors down.

That it was on the Lake Michigan shoreline meant carefree days at the adjacent public beach, the 14th Street Beach, which closed during the 1970s. "We would be down there all the time in the summer," says Sporer Ruetz. "We would just go down the hill and play in the water." The caveat is that, being so close to the sand and looking like an important building, with all of its horizontal lines, other beachgoers often thought their house was where you changed into a swimsuit. "One year, a prankster wrote 'Men' and 'Women' above the two front doors," says Sporer Ruetz, who met the culprit when they confessed at a dinner party many years later. Hertzberg recalls similar disdain from her parents. "People thought this was the changing house for the 14th Street Beach. They would find people changing in their living room."

The Fourth of July parade route goes past the Hardy House. "During the war, it was tanks and jeeps," recalls Sporer Ruetz.

Half-siblings later joined the family when her mother remarried and had children. "It was a wonderful house to grow up in," says Sporer Ruetz. "I didn't realize it was unique. There were so many steps. We used to run up and down them." Years later, she can still remember exactly how many steps, in fact.

Another memory has to do with the family dog, a dachshund. The playroom, below street level and toward the back of the house, was where she birthed a litter of puppies. In that same room, a cubbyhole was where her father stored a bear rug he'd bought in Alaska. Now, as an adult, Sporer Ruetz questions how the dog, with her short legs, managed all those stairs.

Lake Michigan was like her North Star growing up in this house. "It was always just to the left," she says. "I loved living there. It's hard to believe it's over a hundred years old now."

Willard Keland House, Mount Pleasant

Tour info: This is a private residence and not open for tours. Please respect the owners' privacy.

Many kids move around during their childhoods, from home to home, making new friends and enrolling in different schools.

Not Bill Keland. The nearly 5,000-square-foot Willard Keland House—built in 1957—is the only home he lived in until he later moved away as an adult. It was commissioned by his mother, Karen Johnson Boyd, who raised him and his three sisters in the home—even after her divorce from Willard Keland. It features a copper roof and brick exterior. Built-ins are in abundance, such as cabinets and bookcases.

Bill was born in 1956. Today he's a landscape and figurative painter in Arizona, heavily influenced by growing up in a work of art.

"My mother collected art," he says. "There was a lot of art in the house and, of course, the architecture, so it affected me—what's right and what's wrong, and shape and scale."

His mother was the daughter of H. F. Johnson Jr., whose grandfather Samuel Curtis Johnson founded SC Johnson & Son, Inc., in Racine. "My mom grew up at Wingspread," says Keland. "That was the granddaddy of them all when it comes to Prairie-style [homes]." Mark Hertzberg, author of the book *Wright in Racine*, recalls Johnson Boyd's affinity for Wright, too. "She told her father, 'I loved growing up at Wingspread so much,' and wanted a Wright house," he says.

Hertzberg visited the house many times. In fact, he recalls a story told by Johnson Boyd about a time Wright visited. "Karen invites Wright for lunch and Irene Purcell Johnson

[Karen's stepmother, married to her father H. F. Johnson Jr.] said to Karen, 'You know he's going to rearrange your furniture.' Wright said, 'The piano's in the wrong spot for the children.' Karen and William Wesley Peters [Wright's son-in-law and draftsman] winked at each other," says Hertzberg.

The notion of rearranging furniture wasn't out of the question. When Wright visited Wingspread, he spent all night removing Purcell Johnson's artwork, as he felt it didn't fit with the design. Purcell was only offering her stepdaughter a solid prediction, which ended up coming true.

That the Willard Keland House also had such a strong design pedigree meant Wright and his associates visited more than once. "I met Wright as a two- or three-year-old, but I don't remember it too much," says Keland. "I was around a lot of the associates over the years, especially when updates were made." In 1961, a new front-door entry was created, as well as a breezeway to the new garage. This new layout birthed a triangular garden. Also, the carport was transformed into a primary bedroom. Jack Howe, Wright's chief draftsman, managed this project.

Wright's architectural influence was wrapped around Keland like a metaphorical blanket. In addition to falling asleep in a Wright design, he studied during the day at Prairie School, a private school designed by Wright protégé Charles Montooth. His father spent a lot of time in Spring Green as head of the Wisconsin River Development Corporation and even worked with Wright on developing a golf course, restaurant, and ski hill near Wright's estate. Unfortunately, it was never built. Keland also assisted with the purchase of 2,400 acres in 1965 to complete the construction of Riverview Terrace, now Taliesin's visitor center.

Keland recalls the neighborhood he grew up in as tight-knit, with kids playing in the dead-end street and the Root River practically at the back of his house, as the home is cantilevered over a bluff with a greenbelt behind. "We could ride our bikes down there and go fishing,"

says Keland. "It was a real park setting. There's a lot of privacy and a lot of spaces between the homes."

Inside, the house flaunted 25-foot ceilings where, in the living room, a decorated Christmas tree shined every winter. "It was a great entertaining house," he says. "My parents had a lot of parties there." His favorite area of the home was the balcony above the living room, where a bedroom and bath were located. Here, the kids could spy on what was happening downstairs and also glimpse the outdoors through the living room's walls of windows. "It was a dramatic spot, and also an intimate space on the balcony," says Keland.

The home also boasted a playroom for the kids that was much larger than each of the bedrooms; in typical Wright fashion, he encouraged families to spend time together in communal spaces.

Keland and his daughter later bought the house, as Karen Johnson Boyd died in 2016, and her husband, in 2020. As this book was being written, they put it on the market, and the next steward bought it to enjoy.

"It was a really great house to grow up in," says Keland, "with a lot of inside and outside spaces."

Wingspread, Wind Point

Tour info: Free hour-long tours are available 10 a.m., noon, and 2 p.m., Wednesday–Sunday, with advance reservations, and when weddings and conferences are not taking place. wingspread.com

This 36-acre spread in Wind Point, a tiny village hugging Lake Michigan immediately north of Racine, is unique in that it evolved from a family home into a conference center.

The 14,000-square-foot, Prairie-style home with four wings was built in 1939 for H. F. Johnson Jr., the third generation of the Johnson family to head SC Johnson, in Racine. The privately held company manufactures household cleaning and insect control supplies, and has been headquartered in Racine since its 1886 founding. Johnson Jr.'s awareness of Wright's designs came when the architect designed SC Johnson's Administration Building (completed in 1939) and the Research Tower (opened in 1950).

Each wing had a purpose: the primary bedroom, the children's rooms, the kitchen and servants' quarters, and the garage/guestrooms. Unfortunately, Johnson's second wife died during the construction phase, before he moved in with his two children, Karen and Samuel. He wanted to abandon the project but Wright persuaded him to continue. Later, his third wife—film star Irene Purcell—joined the family. However, she was not a fan of Wright's

design. On an overnight visit he reportedly woke at 5 a.m. to remove the furnishings and paintings of hers he abhorred, replacing them with the Japanese prints he'd previously gifted to her husband. Needless to say, he was never invited back. In 1959 the family moved into the adjacent home designed with Purcell's ideas in mind and donated the original house to the Johnson Foundation, which now uses it as a conference center and to host tours for the public.

Like many of Wright's homes, the front door to the original house is concealed, and the entry displays Wright's compression-and-release technique. At 14,000 square feet, it's among Wright's largest residential commissions. It's also the last of the Prairie-style homes he designed. An open concept prevails throughout the ground floor.

Edgar Tafel oversaw the construction of this three-bedroom, three-bath home. Tidewater red cypress was chosen for the exterior because it was known to not rot. There are just over five hundred windows, including walls of windows in many of the rooms, and seven fireplaces in total. "Anywhere there is a fireplace, [Wright] wants you to be," says tour guide Amanda Thurman Ward, about Wright's intentions.

In the Great Room (used as the family's living room, library, and dining room), a four-sided, floor-to-ceiling stone fireplace anchors the space. Unlike many of Wright's other fireplaces, which are angular, this one is tube-shaped and soars to the ceiling. From the outside, the dome effect is very clear, although inside it feels like the ceilings soar up to the sky (they're that high). Each of the 4-by-4-foot squares were tinted Wright's beloved Cherokee Red, for the flooring. Kasota stone, sourced from Minnesota, was used for the mantel as well as the stairs leading to the second floor. Symbolizing the heart of the home, Wright installed a large hanging kettle on one side of the fireplace, which could be used to serve a hot drink if desired. Pinstripe design flooring is similar to that found at Taliesin. It's easy to see here that Wright is encouraging people to ~~~~ ~~~ ~~~~ the open spaces and not lingering on in their rooms, which are cramped and tucked away, not even close to being as cozy as this crackling hearth, with sunlight bouncing around the room, thanks to the walls of windows.

Built with an intention to entertain, a Seeburg Background Music System—normally found only at car dealerships or department stores during this time—was added to the living room, with the ability to hold two hundred 78 rpm records. A patio overlooks the rose garden, in bloom during the early-summer months. The Johnsons also had an outdoor pool installed at the children's request, as they were worried about moving "far away" from their friends in Racine. While the pool served as an enticing invitation to visitors, it wasn't easy to convince Wright to add it to the design, as he reportedly called them "outdoor bathtubs." He compromised with a design that's more like a reflecting pool, measuring 125 feet long and 25 feet wide. An outdoor fireplace allowed for activities such as roasting marshmallows.

Despite their initial hesitation, the kids came to love the house. "Sam [eleven years old when he moved in] said it was like living in a spaceship," says Thurman Ward. Another request from the children was to add a cupola or "crow's nest" to the second story, modeled after a spiral staircase they'd loved at their grandparents' farm. This enabled them to watch their father

fly by in his small, private airplane. Karen, fifteen years old when they moved in, asked for a balcony off her room after seeing one at Taliesin. Due to concerns regarding proper support of this cantilevered feature, her design dream almost didn't happen—until Edgar Tafel, Wright's apprentice, stepped in. He asked Johnson if he'd like a safe for storage; if so, he'd happily install a steel beam coming from it.

No Wright home is perfect, of course, including this one. The final budget was three times what Wright had quoted. From day one, says Thurman Ward, the 190 clerestory windows leaked. In fact, while hosting a dinner party, Johnson Jr. was startled to feel drops of water on his bald head while seated at the dining table with local business leaders and local and state government officials. When he phoned Wright at Taliesin West to complain about the leaking, Wright responded that the only—and best—solution was to move his chair. Another quirk in the design has to do with the dining table. While Wright had already showcased built-in desks and tables, this dining table went a step further by retracting into the kitchen via wheels. The idea was to give Johnson privacy and not have the servants intrude on conversation during mealtime. Unfortunately, this required coordination between those who were in the kitchen and those dining on the other side.

Walking throughout this home, it's easy to notice a few original Wright-designed furnishings and decor, such as barrel chairs and two lamps. A downstairs lamp is undeniably of Wright's design: It's Cherokee Red and boasts a swing arm within a built-in.

The conference center—which now includes a Leadership in Energy and Environmental Design (LEED)–certified guesthouse and forty guestrooms, along with a former garage that serves as the foundation's office—keeps a robust business. A variety of industries have hosted meetings here, and two major organizations—the National Endowment for the Arts and National Public Radio—were conceived here. In 2022 site managers and directors from Wright-designed sites all across the country met here for a conference.

In 1975 Wingspread was listed on the National Register of Historic Places, and was designated a National Historic Landmark in 1989.

DELAVAN AND LAKE GENEVA

A. P. Johnson House, Delavan
Tour info: This is a private residence and not open for tours. Please respect the owners' privacy.

Built for Andrew Johnson, the owner of Johnson Chair Company (a Chicago furniture dealer) and his family in 1905, this Prairie-style home is one of five houses Wright designed along Delavan Lake, all between 1900 and 1905. The other four are the Henry Wallis Cottage (1900); the Fred B. Jones Estate, also known as "Penwern" (1900–03); the George W. Spencer House (1902); and the Charles S. Ross House (1902).

Fitting for this lakefront community, where many of the homes were occupied only during the summer, Wright also designed the Delavan Lake Yacht Club. Built in 1902, it was later demolished in 1916. With its board-and-batten siding and low, hipped roof, it was a characteristic Wright design. Inside was a kitchen, dance floor, dining room, and ladies' parlor.

Holly Campbell moved into this home in 1980 with her husband, James. A barn on the property—not designed by Wright—includes four horse stalls, a tool room, and space formerly used as a kitchen and caretaker's quarters. Like many Wright stewards, it wasn't the fact

that it was a Wright design that enticed them. She grew up in Delavan, and her husband in Janesville. They'd always wanted a home on the lake.

She recalls the February day they first saw the home. It had been vandalized and empty for some time. The picture window was boarded up. "I really didn't know that much about Frank Lloyd Wright. He wasn't as popular then as he is now. [That] it was a Frank Lloyd Wright [design] didn't really mean anything to us. We liked the style of the chimney, its contemporary design and very clean lines," says Campbell.

Despite seeing the obvious beauty, it was apparent a restoration was needed. "We worked on the house for a couple of years," says Campbell. "It really, really was not in good shape at all. No one wanted to tackle it, apparently." Up until then, the house had only been occupied seasonally. The Campbells wanted to live in it full-time.

In 1982, the property was put on the National Register of Historic Places. Then, between 2004 and 2008, the Campbells worked with Taliesin Architects on further projects. This included adding new wood to the exterior and fixing the home's hardwood flooring. "When we bought the house, the floors were sloped," says Campbell. "We had raccoons living under the house." The once-open verandas were enclosed, and a lower level added with a recreation room and guest rooms. The east-facing porch is now the dining room.

"Everything that has been done here was done with Frank Lloyd Wright in mind," says Campbell.

As a steward, Campbell has studied as much as she can about the property's provenance. "It was built strictly as a summer cottage. [Johnson's] family owned it for fifty-seven years. They lived in Chicago during the winter," she says. The Campbells have been in touch with Johnson's descendants, to help fill in the blanks about their years living in the house. This includes Kay Johnson Sweeney, the wife of Andrew's grandson, Art. "I learned a lot talking to Art's wife. She would come out often with the children. She had an old station wagon without windows [that] you had to crank to start," says Campbell.

Art's son Mark was committed to keeping the vehicle in the family. "He took [out] every nut, bolt, and screw and restored that vehicle. One time he took me around the house, around South Shore, at top speed, 40 miles per hour," she says. Art also shared stories about growing

up on the property—especially how a flat spot was perfect for outdoor games. "He said 'My aunts and uncles would play croquet [there].' They'd be out there until dark," says Campbell.

Other factoids she picked up were that the picture window had been brought up from Chicago by horse and wagon, and Roman bricks were chosen by Wright for the fireplace design. Also, a caretaker used to live on the property with the Johnsons, and the main house's kitchen featured a copper sink.

Lake Geneva Public Library, Lake Geneva

Tour info: Open to the public Monday, Friday, and Saturday, 9 a.m.–5 p.m.; and Tuesday–Thursday, 9 a.m.–8 p.m. A self-guided tour can be taken using a free brochure at the front desk. lglibrary.org

One of the best spots for a lake view in this resort town isn't on the beach. Instead, it's perched on a bluff above Lake Geneva Public Beach—in the library. The Prairie-style library was designed by architect James Dresser, a student of Wright's. You can find the redbrick building with its gently sloping roof and Cherokee Red door trim quite easily, as it's nearly a block long, within Library Park.

Fresh off a spring 2022 renovation by FEH Design in Oconomowoc, Wisconsin, walls of windows remain on the library's beachfront side. Stained-glass panel dividers in the study areas don't restrict the view, nor do they cut out the light. These were designed by Gilbertson's Stained-Glass Studio, a local company, and serve as replicas of the pattern of the Geneva Hotel pattern designed by Wright.

New Prairie-style light fixtures hang from the entry's ceiling, as do a pair of stained-glass windows that hung in the Lake Geneva Hotel's upper level. That hotel was built by Wright in 1912 and razed during the winter of 1970, in favor of a Kenosha developer's proposed glossy new building.

An electric fireplace once covered up is now on full view and accessible with the flip of a switch. It's anchored by a redbrick surround and a shorter base, allowing room for two blue Midcentury Modern–style upholstered rockers. In honor of those who donated $1,000 each toward the library's $1 million restoration, faux book spines were added to the floating shelves, depicting either the name of the female donor or a woman the donor admires. To better accommodate modern times, a computer bar (the A. G. Cox Public Computer Area) was added, along with two new meeting rooms designed for small groups. In fact, hanging in the Margaret Smith Meeting Room, on the east wall, is an architectural drawing of the library by James Dresser & Associates, his namesake firm.

During the renovation, changes were made to either improve the library's function or better align with its architectural and historical roots. The original orienting of shelving in the west half of the building was restored. Flooring, plumbing, and air handling systems were all updated. Untouched are nods to Dresser's original design from when the library debuted and was dedicated, in 1954; for example, wood cutouts on a two-story section of the library, and a soaring ceiling at each of the two entrances—one facing the lake, and the other, West Main Street—not unlike what greets you when entering Field's at the Wilderness, a restaurant designed by Dresser in the Wisconsin Dells. Original millwork also remains. The only major aesthetic change to the entry, other than the new light fixtures, was transforming the ceiling's "murky blue," as community engagement librarian Ellen Ward-Packard dubbed it, to a soft, creamy ivory.

This is the only branch for the town's 7,872 year-round residents, which easily balloons during the summer months. It's not the first branch, however. That one opened in 1895, within a cottage donated by Mary Sturges, a local resident who fled to the area after the 1871 Chicago fire.

On a visit, pick up a four-page brochure detailing the library's history, including Dresser's architecture, for a self-guided tour. This was authored by local historian Ginny Hall. One is welcome to poke around the library—quietly, of course—following the brochure's step-by-step commentary of what you see. Used books—a mix of hardcovers and paperbacks—are often sold at the library by the Friends of the Lake Geneva Library. A perfect spot to read on a nice day is on the library's patio, facing the lake. One can also access the famed 21-mile walk around Geneva Lake from just outside the library, winding past historical mansions for a deep dive into this town's historical architecture.

Penwern, Delavan

Tour info: This is a private residence and not open for tours. Please respect the owners' privacy. penwern.com

Although Wright designed five residences on Delavan Lake—plus the Delavan Lake Yacht Club boathouse—between 1900 and 1905, his crown jewel is this one. Referred to as Penwern, it was built between 1900 and 1903 for Fred B. Jones as a summer estate with four separate buildings. The other homes on the lake are the Prairie-style A. P. Johnson House (1905), the Wallis-GoodSmith House (1900), George W. Spencer House (1902), and Charles S. Ross House (1902). Unfortunately, the boathouse was completely destroyed when a new clubhouse was built across the street.

This estate, which was placed on the National Register of Historic Places in 1974, carries a remarkable story of dedicated architectural restoration. In 1994, John and Sue Major bought the property, which then included the main house, boathouse, and stable, which had deteriorated over the years. What followed was twenty-five years of intense restoration, beginning with the stable. A gym was later added, and two offices: one in the former stable hand's office, and another in the former card-playing tower. For the restoration, the couple worked with Bill Orkild of Copenhagen Construction. Another subsequent project meant removing two additions made to the house by Jones, in 1909 and 1910, not part of Wright's original design.

In the early 2000s, the Majors were able to buy the Penwern Gate Lodge, making the estate complete again.

John O'Shea, who served as a steward of Penwern from 1989 to 1994, procured copies of Wright's seventeen drawings of Penwern, proving what the architect ultimately wanted to see. "That's where the Majors realized the additions were in fact additions and not originals, and had them removed," says Mark Hertzberg, author of *Frank Lloyd Wright's Penwern: A Summer Estate.* "John [Major] has talked about going grocery shopping and being lambasted by people for ruining a design by Frank Lloyd Wright when, in fact, it was not by Frank Lloyd Wright."

Throughout the process, the Majors felt it important to bring the estate back to what Wright had wanted. Then, in the main house, the kitchen was updated, along with the upstairs baths.

The Majors purchased the Penwern Gate Lodge, once part of the Penwern estate, from Terry Robbins Canty's children, after Canty's death. Canty's parents, Burr and Peg Robbins, were the second stewards of Penwern. "They restored [it] to the original [design]," says Hertzberg about the Majors. "There were two greenhouses at the Gate Lodge—both commercially built. One was in Wright's plans. He has it in his drawing and he cited it—attached to the water tower, with a boulder wall attached to it. Fred Jones loved growing roses." In 2020, the Majors undid the work of previous stewards at the Gate Lodge, by bringing back the greenhouse where the original one had been, and adopting the same footprint. It's not the type of greenhouse where you'd pot plants or start plants from seed, however; it's more ornate than this. "It's a place for them to entertain friends," says Hertzberg.

Other work to the Gate Lodge included adding two and a half baths, repairing water damage, enclosing the back porch, repairing damaged stucco walls, and rebuilding the eaves.

Throughout the process, the Majors have been intentional about showcasing the history of this property to anyone who visits. While Penwern is not open to the public, they do host friends and family, and, in June 2022, the Frank Lloyd Wright Building Conservancy hosted a fund-raising dinner here.

The final piece in this long, complex restoration proved to be the most controversial. In order to fully realize Wright's design, the estate needed a boathouse, like the one found in the drawings. One was on the site, but due to a 1978 arson fire, it was in major disrepair and could no longer be used. The Majors opted to rebuild on the existing foundation, hiring a restoration architect to follow Wright's original drawings. Some in the community felt it would be appropriate to re-create the boathouse design Wright had intended. Still others fought tooth and nail for the boathouse to never be built.

"The town of Delavan did not want to give permission to rebuild the boathouse," says Hertzberg, and the Wisconsin Department of Natural Resources did not want "new" boathouse structures built on the lake, "but the Majors didn't give up." Since the boathouse had not been used in more than a year, despite the Majors' insistence they did use it—to store water toys and provide access to the pier—this meant the prospect of rebuilding was dead in the water.

Brian Spencer rallied the troops and got forty-six Wright scholars, historians, and architects, plus Wright's grandson, Eric Lloyd Wright, to pen letters of support. Eventually the Walworth County Zoning Agency reversed its decision. The boathouse could legally be rebuilt on the original site. Key to winning the fight was proving this was an original structure and, therefore, did not have to conform to existing ordinances for new-build structures.

"They have brought Penwern back," says Hertzberg. "They've done a heroic restoration. Building the boathouse was Herculean, but a lot of it is stabilizing the estate. If the Majors had not come along, and someone else had bought it, the [non-Wright] additions [to the house] would still be there. That's the most significant thing. The Gate Lodge would not have been restored and the boathouse rebuilt."

One example of their attention to detail is in the weather vane flanking the fireplace in the main house. Depicting Fred B. Jones's initials, it's the exact weather vane that once stood atop the stable's roof. The Majors brought that one inside, to preserve it as much as possible, and commissioned a replica to go back on the roof. "That speaks to their commitment to the vision that Fred B. Jones and Frank Lloyd Wright had," says Hertzberg.

Lake Geneva Hotel, Lake Geneva
Tour info: This building is no longer standing as the result of its 1970 demolition.

In a resort town like Lake Geneva, it's difficult to fathom why a hotel that drew people for the lake views and a respite from city life would ever be torn down.

Especially a hotel designed by Wright.

But that's exactly what happened, on a frigid February day in 1970.

Helen Brandt was a new resident at the time, enticed from the North Woods for a job at the Lake Geneva Public Library. She remembers standing along the lakefront and watching the hotel collapse. The site is a block south of Main Street and along Center Street. Continuing south, Center Street runs into Wrigley Drive and Geneva Lake's glittery shoreline in two blocks. Plans for a $5 million resort complex from a Kenosha businessman had won people over, more than saving what had become a struggling hotel. Only one tower was ever built. It's now called Geneva Tower.

"It was very sad," says Brandt. "There did not seem to be any opposition to the fact that a Frank Lloyd Wright building was going down. The words 'historic preservation' were not in our vocabulary." Brandt estimates she was one of about twenty-five people who witnessed the wrecking ball. Today, of course, due to rising acclaim for Wright's designs, there would be thousands in attendance, along with every major media outlet—that is, if the proposal to tear it down hadn't already been stopped.

With a large fireplace in the lobby along with low, hipped roofs and bands of windows, this two-story hotel was uncharacteristically a Wright design. It also featured an overhanging red cantilevered roof, a favorite design feature of Wright's, paired with a cream-colored exterior. "Banks of leaded-glass windows stretched from Broad Street to Center Street," according to a

HOTEL GENEVA, LAKE GENEVA, WIS.

March/April 1988 article by Ted Schaefer in *Lake Geneva* magazine. In the dining room was a multicolored glass ceiling as eye-catching as Wright's leaded-glass windows.

Unfortunately, the hotel closed in 1966.

But when it was first built in 1912, the hotel was well received. It replaced the Whiting House Hotel, which had burned down in 1894. It had been a four-story, wood-frame, Elizabethan-style structure. It was known for having "lavish rooms, wide outside porches, and a 'sky parlor'—a dancing hall on the fourth floor. Its crystal chandeliers, thickly carpeted hallways, and such extra facilities as a barber shop and billiards room marked it as perhaps the most luxurious hotel of its time in Wisconsin," wrote Schaefer.

In 1911, local businessman John Williams and developer Arthur L. Richards commissioned Wright for the design of a new hotel on the site. This was around the same time Wright worked with Richards on the American System-Built Homes. Their reasons for embarking on a hotel project were clear: Only two hotels existed in Lake Geneva at that time, Hotel Florence and Hotel Denison. And yet many people were traveling here, particularly during the summer months, and they needed a place to stay. A three-story residential wing Wright designed was never built, but appears to be a precursor to luxury hotel brands today. Many in Lake Geneva, such as Grand Geneva Resort & Spa or The Abbey, branch out into real estate, promising buyers a resort-like lifestyle from the comfort of their condos or private homes on the property.

Over time, the hotel bore three names: Hotel Geneva, Geneva Inn, and Lake Geneva Hotel. It was last owned by Sen. Richard Borg, between 1967 and when it came down; and before that, Hobart Hermansen, E. T. Nussbaum, A. H. Thierback, and B. K. Thierback. The Taffy Twist Lounge was popular with guests and locals, says Geneva Lake Museum executive

director Janet Ewing. She's familiar with Wright's work, having grown up in River Forest, Illinois, home to several of his residential commissions. Ewing also heard many stories about the hotel from her parents. "I know my dad was furious," she says, when it was announced the hotel would be torn down. "I was just a little kid. I don't remember the hotel. I must have driven past it."

Tulip designs within second-story, art-glass windows were unique to the hotel. The ground-floor windows featured a geometric design. There was also a stained-glass skylight designed by Wright in the lobby that served as a source of beauty but also invited in natural light. A wood-burning brick fireplace with a sunburst-style hearth in the lobby, with two built-in upholstered benches on each side, is featured in many of the historic photos that remain. Because every resort town's hotel should have a pool, this one did, too: a sunken, kidney-shaped design, outdoors.

Wright and his third wife, Olgivanna, reportedly visited the hotel often and stayed overnight, enjoying lunch or dinner on-site. Reviews while the hotel was open were mixed. Roof overhangs made many of the rooms feel dark. People came to Lake Geneva—and still do today—for the wide-open lake and bright light, not cozy-but-cramped quarters. And, like most of Wright's homes, bedrooms weren't a focus. "I've talked to people over the years who said the rooms were very small," says Brandt.

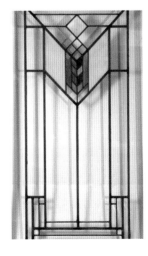

In an era before Tripadvisor reviews, however, people still checked in. At one point the hotel restaurant morphed into serving Cantonese cuisine, made popular during this time period, as many servicemen had served in the South Pacific and were now back home. A vintage, laminated menu preserved from the hotel shows everything from a fresh shrimp cocktail (75 cents) to "fancy corned beef" ($1). Iced coffee or

tea was a whopping 15 cents. As a nod to this era's fascination with tropical life in the South Pacific, two of the cocktails are planters punch and Singapore sling. Another appeal to hotel guests is that the lake couldn't be any closer, but was also two blocks away, which helped to cultivate its own identity away from the hustle and bustle.

Like today, Lake Geneva was a playground for restless Chicagoans yearning for respite in a small, quiet town and access to nature—along with opportunities to dine out and socialize. Checking into Wright's hotel fit into that vision. "It's always been a vacation mecca for the Chicagoans," says Ewing. "When the railroad was built [in July 1871], it got crazy. When the Great Chicago Fire happened [in October 1871], it got even crazier."

Today Brandt's a curator at Geneva Lake Museum. In 1967, there were only two librarian jobs open in the state of Wisconsin, and Lake Geneva was one of them. Brandt took a leap and moved south, open to whatever adventures happened next, and hoping one day to return home. "My father had just died. I was only going to stay two years. This July [2022], I will have been here fifty years," says Brandt.

A permanent exhibit in the museum, in downtown Lake Geneva, houses relics that include dinnerware (china and silverware), a stained-glass reading lamp, a leaded-glass window, and stained-glass sconces. Considering it's no longer possible to visit the hotel, due to its demise, popping into the museum to learn more about this design is the next best option.

A. B. Groves Building Co. House, Madison

Tour info: This is a private residence and not open for tours. Please respect the owners' privacy.

In 2019, Erica Diehl and her husband, Scott, along with their elderly cat, Fletcher, were on the hunt for a larger home in their Madison neighborhood. Snapping up a recently discovered 1917 Frank Lloyd Wright house three blocks away was never part of the plan.

"It's just 'our house,'" says Diehl, adding that 95 percent of their decision to put in an offer on the three-bedroom, two-bath home came down to the neighborhood. "We prefer to commute by walking or biking. We have one car we use maybe once a week."

But still, the couple was attracted to the American System-Built Home's natural light, the gardening space, and the fact that two home offices could easily be accommodated, as well as the 2,450-square-foot floor plan and its built-in storage throughout.

They quickly embarked on a few functional improvements and maintenance projects, with an eye toward restoring the home back to the way Wright intended it to be. One such project was removing a rotting porch on a back addition that was not part of the original drawings.

"It's very leaky," says Diehl. "If we have a rainstorm, [the porch] basically floods."

Once properly insulated, the new enclosed porch will remain cozy year-round. "We are very cognizant of the fact that it's a one-hundred-year-old home with historical features," says

Diehl. To that end, the couple kept the porch's transom leaded-glass windows while replicating only those below, so they are the right dimensions for the new porch design.

Original leaded-glass windows that also often leaked were repaired by a local company. They also added insulation to the attic. Throughout the process they asked questions of John Waters, preservation programs manager at the Frank Lloyd Wright Building Conservancy in Chicago.

Thankfully, the previous owner, who lived there for thirty years, had already done a lot of restoration work. Linda McQuillen was also the owner when it was revealed by a Wright historian in 2015 that this is an American System-Built Home—one of the prototypes, in fact.

Mary Jane Hamilton reportedly documented her findings about the home over a twenty-year period, conferring with Mike Lilek, who also led the documentation of the Elizabeth Murphy House in Shorewood, and serves as curator of Frank Lloyd Wright's Burnham Block in Milwaukee. Connecting with the twenty owners of Wright's other American System-Built Homes—of which only twenty-five were completed, despite more than 900 drawings—has been a huge help. "People who own ASB Homes have a lot of similar issues," Diehl says, "so seeing people delve into their discoveries and mysteries is helpful."

"It's a very solidly built house. All of the improvements we're making are not very structural, porch aside. Hopefully this will last beyond the time we are here," says Diehl.

First Unitarian Society Meeting House, Shorewood Hills

Tour info: Public tours offered May–October by the Friends of the Meeting House. A 10:10 a.m. Sunday tour immediately follows the 9 a.m. service during the school year, and a 9 a.m. tour precedes the 10 a.m. service during summer. There is no cost to attend services, and the Landmark Auditorium is open to the public weekdays between 10 a.m. and 2 p.m. Tickets for public tours must be purchased online 24 hours in advance. fusmadison.org and unitarianmeetinghouse.org

While Frank Lloyd Wright designed ten churches, only two are in Wisconsin: the saucer-shaped Annunciation Greek Orthodox Church in Wauwatosa, Wisconsin; and the triangle-shaped First Unitarian Society Meeting House in the Madison suburb of Shorewood Hills.

What makes this Unitarian congregation—among the country's largest, with just over one thousand members—unique is that Wright himself was a member. He knew very well the parishioners who commissioned his design in 1946. He also understood the format of each service, which helped in making decisions about placement of windows, seating, and other furnishings. You might even argue that he knew the likes and dislikes of his fellow congregants regarding design.

Still, he had a vision. The triangle-shaped church—with a prow extending off the Meeting House (sanctuary)—would be like no other house of worship in its design.

"It's a wonderful feeling in this church because it's not ornate," says March Schweitzer, a member who gives tours of the church, completed in 1951. Construction began in 1949. "It has a very peaceful feeling." Despite being referred to around town as "Frank Lloyd Wrong,"

Schweitzer says—he was known for not paying his bill at restaurants or walking out of Manchester's Department Store with a stack of dress shirts he hadn't paid for—his own congregation picked him to design their new church.

Wright grew up in a religious family and therefore had been surrounded by dialogue about morals and ethics. His father was a minister, and Wright's early childhood was spent moving around Iowa, Massachusetts, and Rhode Island to his father's various parishes. During the late 1870s the family settled in Madison and became founding members of the First Unitarian Society Meeting House at its original location, in downtown Madison. (The facility they built was later demolished, in favor of a parking lot, providing funds for the new church.)

From the outside, it's clear this is an example of Wright's Usonian-style architecture when you see the bands of clerestory windows and long sight lines. The door is nearly concealed beneath low eaves, just the way Wright liked it. The dolomitic limestone exterior was sourced from a quarry in Wisconsin's Driftless Area. Inside, Wright employed radiant floor heating—appealing for cold Sunday mornings in Wisconsin—and his beloved Cherokee Red is found throughout. Recessed lighting was also employed. A fireplace in the Meeting House is no longer used, but at one time provided a crackling backdrop. In the entry sits one of his bench designs. Also on-site are Wright-designed triangular tables and a curtain panel, and a faux bell originally hung in the prow.

"It's one of Frank Lloyd Wright's seventeen most important buildings, named by the American Institute of Architects in 1964," says Schweitzer. (This list also includes Fallingwater in Pennsylvania.) "It has had a profound impact on church organizations in the twentieth century [in moving] away from rectangular buildings with steeples," she says. In 2004 the church became a National Historic Landmark.

"Wright called this his 'little country church,'" says Schweitzer. Set on 4.5 acres, it was not surrounded by UW Health buildings and strip malls as it is now. The church's only neighbors at the time were the UW–Madison agricultural-sciences buildings.

Another distinguishing difference is the lack of stained-glass windows. "He was always trying to bring the outside in," says Schweitzer, "so there [are] no colored windows." These would, of course, block sunlight.

The initial quote was $60,000, but costs quickly soared to $80,000. Then, contractors quoted between $350,000 and $700,000. "It looked like it wasn't going to be built, but Wright wanted his church to be built," says Schweitzer.

Wright found an ally in Marshall Erdman, who quoted $102,000, which the 150 congregants felt they could afford. Chipping in with labor, many volunteered to haul the 1,000 tons of dolomite from a quarry 40 miles away. Ladies in the church wove the Meeting House Curtain at Taliesin, and it still hangs today. The final price for this church: $220,000.

No one could have expected how much the design would capture the community's interest, as well as visiting architects from around the world. A two-person staff—just the minister and a receptionist—could not handle incessant knocks on the door for "just a quick tour." They hired a high-school student to lead tours, charging 50 cents each.

"Wright said 'Charge them a dollar,'" said Schweitzer.

Congregants criticized the low entryway, but Wright had a retort. "Let them bow their heads," he said. Still, when his son-in-law hit his head, he immediately fixed it.

A sawtooth-style wall hosts doors to classrooms that are now church offices. Twelve Utagawa Hiroshige prints presented to the church by Wright are hung here, too. "He gave us all these prints at cost and told us precisely where they were to be hung," says Schweitzer.

In 1964 a wing in Wright's drawings was finally realized by Taliesin architect William Wesley Peters. "It's really cozy to be in here for a meeting with the fireplace going, [when] it's snowing outside," says Schweitzer.

Then, in 1964, a new wing, part of Wright's original design, was finally realized. This was followed by a second addition in 1992. But the most acclaimed one came in 2008, when Kubala Washatko Architects designed a 20,000-square-foot addition from scratch—but in the vein of Wright's designs. It immediately earned LEED-certified Silver status, and quickly expanded to embody the Gold status. Sixteen geothermal wells are located beneath the parking lot. Sconces were born out of recycled copper left over from a revamp to the roof, which is now a green roof, sprouting grass each spring. Rarely do light switches need to be flicked on during the daytime thanks to an abundance of windows coaxing in natural light.

Every Friday at noon classical-music concerts take place in the five-hundred-seat auditorium. These are free for the community. This is also an homage to the benefit concerts once hosted in the sanctuary during Wright's era, to raise money for the church. Weddings, too, are hosted in the new addition.

"Building a historical landmark is a big feat, but building a Frank Lloyd Wright historical landmark is [a different] order of magnitude," says Schweitzer.

Herbert and Katherine Jacobs I House, Madison
Tour info: This is a private residence and not open for tours. Please respect the owners' privacy.

As a renowned professor emeritus of art history, Jim Dennis knows beauty when he sees it. And the first time he spotted this 1,550-square-foot Usonian-style home, he fell in love.

His first introduction to the house, built in 1937, was on a whim. In 1982 he suggested to one of his students, Brad Lynch, they drive by a Wright-designed home he'd heard about. When Dennis glimpsed the "for sale" sign in the yard, his heart skipped a beat. Could this be his next home?

Dennis bought the house with his wife and quickly recruited Lynch to assist with restoring the home. Jobs included removing a retaining wall and rebuilding the carport, part of the original design. Next, 2-by-4-foot Cherokee Red tiles were added as flooring. "It's the right color now," says Dennis.

Interestingly, Lynch is now a practicing architect with experience restoring other Wright homes, in addition to the Jacobs House. Two of Dennis's other students—Jonathan Leck and John Eifler—also assisted with this massive makeover. Like Lynch, they both have made a career out of restoring Wright homes around the country. Leck even crafts lamps based on his

own designs, as well as those of Wright. One of those designs serves as Dennis's reading lamp atop a desk in the living room that's original to the house.

This Usonian flaunts three firsts for Wright: a carport, radiant floor heating, and usage of track lighting. It was also Wright's first Usonian design. The home was built for Herbert and Katherine Jacobs, but the couple resided in the home for only six years before building the second Jacobs House designed by Wright, 6 miles away, then moving to California. Herbert was a prominent journalist in Madison, writing for the *Capital Times*, and later taught at the University of California, Berkeley's journalism school. Dennis is the seventh owner.

Dennis was fortunate to have seen Wright at least once, at one of his lectures, in 1958. Dennis also knew Olgivanna, Wright's third wife, after Wright died. Coincidentally, Dennis's aunt back in his home state of Ohio also met Wright when he spoke to her garden club. Had they met later, he might even have remembered her, because she challenged a comment he made about historic homes, disparaging them.

Over the years, Dennis has acquired some of Wright's furnishings, including a dining chair next to the writing desk. The dining table he brought back into the home, too. A large black-and-white framed photo of Wright with the poet Carl Sandburg hangs in the bath.

While beautiful and a living work of art, the home has had its issues.

"The problem was the roof. It leaked so badly," says Dennis. He recalls phoning a California redwoods group to inquire about ponderosa wood to repair the damaged ceiling. "Lo and behold, she was from Wisconsin. I asked her, 'Do you like Frank Lloyd Wright?' She said, 'I love Frank Lloyd Wright,' and I thought, 'Man, I'm in.'"

Dennis has carved out his own eclectic style within, such as lining the living room's built-in ponderosa pine and redwood shelving with his collection of art books, including copies of his own titles: *Renegade Regionalists: The Modern Independence of Grant Wood, Thomas Hart*

Benton, and John Steuart Curry; Robert Koehler's The Strike: *The Improbable Story of an Iconic 1886 Painting of Labor Protest*; and *Karl Bitter: Architectural Sculptor, 1867–1915*. He also appears to own nearly every book written about Frank Lloyd Wright, with *New Yorker* journalist Brendan Gill's *Many Masks: A Life of Frank Lloyd Wright* a favorite.

In one corner of the living room, his guitar rests for impromptu playing of what he dubs "hillbilly country music." Hung on the walls are landscape paintings by Dennis, along with etchings by prominent printmaker Warrington Colescott, a good friend of Dennis's until his 2018 death. A Guggenheim etching by France Meyer is a nod to one of Wright's other designs.

Iowan painter Grant Wood—his most famous work, *American Gothic* (1930), now hangs in the Art Institute of Chicago—is the subject of many of Dennis's writings and studies. In fact, an upholstered chair and ottoman set designed by Wood rests proudly in the living room, facing the fireplace.

Katherine Jacobs designed triangular cutout lights above the dining table, in a nook just off the kitchen. On a sunny day they create patterns on the walls and floor.

In the back of the house, a study features more shelves of books. But it's not where Dennis can write well. Or at all. "This is the study," he says, not hiding the irony of these words. "Herbert [Jacobs] said 'I never wrote a line [in here]. I sat in the living room with a typewriter.'"

These days, Dennis is working on an architectural memoir, and enjoys sitting down at the writing desk in the living room, listening to classical music as he types away on a laptop.

Herbert and Katherine Jacobs II House, Middleton
Tour info: This is a private residence and not open for tours. Please respect the owners' privacy.

Betty and John Moore wanted an "interesting" house. Their Cape Cod in Ann Arbor, Michigan, with its angular, cramped rooms, didn't cut it. After selling that home, they lived for a blissful year along a pond in a modern house near the Eastern Michigan University campus, where John taught chemistry and Betty was on the chemistry staff. They had also owned a one-story modern home in Bloomington, Indiana. Then the University of Wisconsin–Madison called with job offers. Would they be willing to move to Madison?

That was in 1989. Their hunt for an "interesting" house led them to this Wright-designed solar hemicycle, an example of passive solar design. It's built in a full half-circle plan. Radiant floor heating, a flat roof, and concrete floors are three key features that reduce reliance on utilities by embracing the earth's energy. Also, the angle of the roof overhang allows for sunshine to flood the house in winter but, come summer, protects the rooms from harsh rays.

Built and designed into a grassy hill between 1944 and 1948, many people, including the university's department chair, advised the couple not to buy this Wright-designed home when it came on the market. There were rumors it had fallen into disrepair, and besides, everyone knew that if you bought a Wright home you'd be spending a lot to restore it. Another chemistry professor had gone to high school with the daughters of the home's original stewards and had heard rumblings of its lack of upkeep. Also, Wright "was very unpopular in Madison, for not paying his bills," says Betty. But his image with Madisonians was starting to change. In fact, soon after they moved in, the Realtor saw a wall-size photo of this very home at a Museum of Science and Industry exhibit in Chicago about Wright's Usonian homes, *Frank Lloyd Wright's Ideas and Treasures.* "Apparently, she exclaimed 'I sold that house!'" says John Moore.

There was another reason for the hesitation. It had been on the market for almost five years. Why hadn't anyone snapped up this 2,650-square-foot architectural beauty? Spruce

wood adorns the roof, second floor and supporting beams. Some of the walls were crafted from 440 tons of limestone sourced a few miles away.

Back at the University of Michigan, the Moores scrounged up two copies of a book about the house, authored by Herbert and Katherine Jacobs: *Building with Frank Lloyd Wright: An Illustrated Memoir* (published in 1978). "Each of us sat [in the library] and read a copy," recalls Betty.

Ultimately, the feeling that they'd be moving into a money pit didn't stop the Moores from putting in an offer. As it turns out, the second family to have owned this home (the Taylors) had embarked on updates before putting it on the market. That was the work of Bill Taylor, one of the children, who purchased the home from his mother. He'd reinforced the roof over-hangs, strengthened the roof, torn up the concrete floor with a jackhammer to replace it (along with the radiant floor heating), replaced the curved wall of windows, and added insulation. The south-facing window wall was upgraded to insulated windows, and forced-air heating and air-conditioning were added upstairs for further comfort. Five new skylights were added to the second floor, drawing in even more natural light, and bringing the total to seven.

"We wanted a house to move into, not a house to fix up," says John. "If he hadn't fixed it up, it wouldn't be here."

In 2005 the Moores rebuilt a detached studio on the property, used to host visiting faculty overnight. An original limestone wall remains, and there's also a carport, storage area, garage, and workshop area. In 2008 the structure's design won a preservation award from the Madison Trust for Historic Preservation. The house's open layout, including a suspended balcony between the two levels, has been conducive to hosting department parties each fall. "You can use the inside and the outside and the kids can run around," says Betty.

As for the wall of sconces in the living room, each bore a pull string that Bill Taylor upgraded to a single light switch, which made turning the lights on or off a time-consuming task. They eventually upgraded to light switches in each, and then an electronic remote control for all. It was after they arrived home to a dark room with a visiting professor, fumbling to turn the lights on, that they knew something had to give.

"When we moved in," recalls Betty, "it rained the first night and the roof leaked. The next day people came from Germany." These tourists wanted to see the house, but the Moores were sleep-deprived and exhausted. Now, when Wright fans arrive, if they're in the yard gardening they'll often invite them to walk around the property. Thankfully, during winter the icy driveway is a deterrent for uninvited visitors.

Originally the Usonian's second floor featured five bedrooms. Now there are three bedrooms and an office/study area. There is just one bath in the home, but it is spacious. A sunken garden in the living room was once a shallow pond. The Moores chose to turn it into an indoor garden instead, with potted cacti and other plants. Besides, "when you're in the house, you're not separated from the outside," says Betty, thanks to Wright's thoughtful, organic design.

As the third owners, they've have been in contact with the Taylors' four surviving children, who lived in the home after the Jacobs family, as well as the three Jacobs children, who are now grown. Seeking a "country retreat" from their Wright-designed home on Madison's west side, Herbert and Katherine Jacobs commissioned him to build this property in what is

now Middleton. While the street is lined with few houses now, when the Moores moved in there were fewer still. For a Usonian, the kitchen is large, eschewing a galley style or cramped quarters (like what's in the Jacobs I House). This is because Katherine did a lot of canning and preserving with the fruits and vegetables harvested from the property. "We met someone who had milked the cows when the Jacobs[es] were here," says Betty.

Minus the animals, the Moores are continuing that tradition on what is now just over 5 acres (the original lot size was closer to 18 acres). They tend a huge garden and, in a modern twist, have added contemporary sculptures in and surrounding the sunken garden, in view just outside the living room. Upon entering the driveway on this dead-end street, a plaque adorning a flagstone declares this a National Historic Landmark building (earned in 2003). Then, a few feet later, another flagstone features a plaque announcing a 1993 Landmark Designation by the Madison Landmarks Commission. They also honor the home's first stewards— Herbert and Katherine Jacobs—through furnishings made by Herbert: a dining-room table, ottomans, built-in cabinets, a kitchen table, and three side tables. All are in the spirit of Wright and could easily be mistaken for his own designs.

Looking around the home, it's easy to see this is a good fit for the Moores. All of the Mid-century Modern furnishings the couple has owned for decades, bought during a postdoc year in Copenhagen, and kept in their past homes, have finally found their place. There are also dozens of Wright books, a testament to their love for the architect's work.

John C. Pew House, Shorewood Hills

Tour info: This is a private residence and not open for tours. Please respect the owners' privacy.

This 1,600-square-foot Usonian home in a Madison suburb is often called "a poor man's Fallingwater." Of course, at the Mill Run, Pennsylvania, marvel, instead of building next to the waterfall, Wright placed the Kaufmanns' home on top of it.

But, says owner Eliot Butler, Wright had a retort for that harsh critique: "Fallingwater is a rich man's Pew House." It's also worth noting that Fallingwater is "grand" for its size. Fallingwater's guesthouse alone is 1,700 feet, on par with the three-bedroom, one-and-a-half bath Pew House's total size.

Still, you can't deny similarities between the two. "It's more like Fallingwater in that it's matched to the site. It cantilevers over a ravine," says Butler.

The Pew House's exterior appears to be carved right into the hillside and resembles a houseboat where the terrace hangs above the lake. Subtle details throughout are a nod to nautical life, but with a Wrightian twist, including square porthole windows and a galley-style kitchen. Like Wright's home in Oak Park, Illinois, a tree grows right through the roof—on

the terrace overlooking Lake Mendota. Standing in the corner of the terrace feels like being on the prow of a boat, says Butler. "There's not a flat wall in the house," says Butler. One of his favorite features is trim on a pillar in the living room, which tapers toward the top and reminds him of Art Deco architecture and, more specifically, the Chrysler Building in his home state of New York. Like Wright's other Usonians, built-in shelves and recessed lighting are found throughout.

Built for John Pew, a Madison businessman, in 1940, the home sits on 75 feet of waterfront. Red tidewater cypress (a favorite material of Wright's) and locally quarried, rough-cut limestone were used in its construction. Inside, features that clearly embody central tenets of Wright's designs include a banquette with storage beneath in the living room, pullout drawers in the bedrooms, and a balcony on the back of the house. Built-in desks are in two of the bedrooms and the living room. Flagstone flooring and stone countertops are also part of the original design, unaltered since their construction.

Butler moved to Madison in 1992 and became a first-time homeowner when he bought this house in 2006. "The first thing that attracted me to the [property] was the home itself," he says. "I wanted to live on the water. When I encountered the house, it was so special compared to other houses I'd seen. It felt like it was the correct house for me."

Butler is the third owner. The previous owners—Cindy and Jon Edwards—moved in during the 1980s. They updated the kitchen, crucial, as Cindy worked as a professional baker, and carpeted the stairs leading to the second floor. "Cindy had been entertaining people [to buy the house] who were fans of Wright or architects but weren't necessarily going to live in the house," says Butler. "They wanted someone who would get use out of it and be a steward."

Butler's parents flew in from New York to check out the house, holding concerns like any parents of first-time homeowners might about buying an old home. Here's what he told them: "Mom and Dad, you don't change a Wright house. A Wright house changes you."

Indeed, it has. While Butler was somewhat familiar with Wright before buying the house, his curiosity only deepened as he read and studied all he could. One of his wedding gifts was an architectural drawing of the home by Wright or one of his draftsmen, now framed and hung on the wall. Throughout the home are other nods to Wright, such as a 1949 Origami Chair his parents found in New York, and an armoire and two glass-top side tables designed by Madison furniture-maker Kevin Early. Jon Edwards built chairs to match a Wright-designed dining table. One of the two bedroom nightstands is original to the home. All of the

floorboards are original. There's also radiant floor heating. "In the winter, it's really cozy," says Butler. In fact, the literal light in the home is incredible during the late afternoons, a tribute to Wright's organic and thoughtful architecture. "The wood captures the light. It just lights up, really golden," says Butler.

That said, there are a few flaws. For one, there's no air-conditioning, although lake breezes and Madison's Upper Midwest climate reduce the impact of hot, sticky summer days. "It's not the easiest house to live in," Butler admits. "There's a lot of storage but it's not immediately accessible," says Butler. "The driveway's long and steep. It gets icy."

To help make it his own, Butler invested in some updates, including adding new kitchen appliances, ensuring all windows and doors open and close property, updating an upstairs bath, and removing marine paint from the terraces. Peter Rott, an architect hired by Butler, is a principal with Isthmus Architecture in Madison and received a Wright Spirit Award from the Frank Lloyd Wright Building Conservancy in 2013 for his work on preserving Wright's projects. In addition to the Pew House, they include Monona Terrace Community and Convention Center, the A. D. German Warehouse, the E. Clarke and Julia Arnold House, and the First Unitarian Society Meeting House.

In 2010 the Pew House received a Historic Preservation Award from the Madison Trust for Historic Preservation. It's also on Wisconsin's State Register of Historic Places.

Even though Butler is not the first to live in this house, "I really feel like it was [meant] for me," he says. At 5-foot-5, he's only 2 inches shorter than Wright, and knows quite well that "there were plenty of places [Wright] had to duck."

He also feels united with Wright in a very keen way when he looks out at Lake Mendota from inside his home. "Wright wanted to build on his boyhood lake," says Butler. "They came for picnics when he was young." In fact, his First Unitarian Society Meeting House is also in Shorewood Hills, only 1.5 miles from the Pew House.

Monona Terrace Community and Convention Center, Madison

Tour info: While the building is open to the public from 8 a.m. to 10 p.m., guided tours are offered for a fee, with advance tickets sold online. mononaterrace.com

With its white, curved lines, this multilevel convention center hugging Lake Monona in downtown Madison bears a keen resemblance to the Guggenheim Museum in New York City. On a warm summer day bicyclists and joggers zip past, enchanted by the lake views, but even on one of Madison's chilliest days, the ice-covered lake is a sight to be seen. Concerts on the rooftop are a popular occurrence on some summer evenings.

As a means to connect Lake Monona with the State Capitol Building, Wright designed this structure off and on between 1938 and 1959, but it wasn't built until 1997, thirty-eight years after his death. However, the connection between Wright and the modern-day construction could not have been stronger. Wright apprentice Anthony Puttnam of Taliesin Architects oversaw the project, which is as true to Wright's original design as humanly possible.

Perched 90 feet over the lake, and owned by the city of Madison, the convention center's meeting rooms and ballrooms are used as a host site for meetings, including the 2022 World

Championship Cheese Contest, and weddings and prom nights, too. Boardrooms can also be used for business meetings. On a guided walking tour of the interior spaces, one gets to see nearly all of the public spaces, provided the rooms aren't booked or being used. Another fun stop is to view furnishings and decor designed by Wright and stored in glass-enclosed cases. This includes a spindle-back chair designed for the David Wright Residence in Phoenix, a barrel chair designed for Wingspread, and china used at the Imperial Hotel in Tokyo, Japan. One of three known busts of Wright is also on display in this area, as is a set of Froebel blocks, designed by Friedrich Froebel, that influenced Wright's design.

And, true to the original intent, an auditorium is part of the final product. A deep red covers each upholstered chair and the curtains are in the same hue. Films, small concerts, and architectural-design talks are hosted here. Not much has changed in the convention center since 1997, given that the building is not that old, or certainly not as old as Wright's other Wisconsin designs. Now on its third carpet design, due to the wear and tear of thousands who have passed through, the current version features ginkgo leaves. Wright fans might recall the gingko tree in front of his Oak Park, Illinois, home and studio.

"It [was] a labor of love for [Wright]," says Heather Sabin, tourism coordinator and frequent tour guide at the 250,000-square-foot convention center. Puttnam also receives endless praise. "Tony really wanted to hit you over the head with the geometry," says Sabin, referring to the spheres that, once you start looking, you see everywhere. Standing in the Grand Terrace, you can't deny the lake's beauty as seen through seven framed windows in each bank within the curved window wall. "He was giving you a platform to view the lake," says Sabin, referring to both Wright's and Puttnam's design decisions.

In addition to the Lecture Hall, Wright's first design also featured a rail depot, courthouse, city hall, and marina. Another design featured spires that, when lit up at night, reminded

people of Morocco or a circus, depending on who you asked. Wright said these circles in the original design were inspired by the State Capitol's dome a few blocks away. At one point, a design also featured a car drive. Wright created eight different designs for the auditorium, with the last right before he died, in April 1959.

In 1938, what local newspapers called "the Dream Civic Center" (not based on Wright's design) was defeated—by a single vote on the Dane County Board. Three years later, Wright tried again. Madison voters had just approved funding for an auditorium, so he resubmitted his plans, with a few modifications. Then, with World War II, the project came to a screeching halt before ground was even broken. Finally, with the war now in the rearview mirror, a 1954 $4 million bond referendum in the city of Madison posed three questions to voters about a proposed auditorium: Should one be built? Should it be on the lakeshore? and Should Frank Lloyd Wright serve as architect? While it did pass, a state legislator reportedly not fond of Wright pushed through a law in 1957 banning any lakefront building on this site taller than 20 feet, placing this project on pause. Wright still did not give up. In 1959, although this was the year Wright died, the law was repealed, paving the way for this project's completion.

In 1967 Taliesin Architects submitted a master plan, but construction bids were deemed over budget, and then-mayor Otto Festge halted the project.

It was clear the city did want an auditorium. But who would build it? In 1989 and 1990, Madison mayor Paul Soglin encouraged the city to revive Wright's design by tweaking it into a convention center, and two years later, voters agreed. Final cost for the project was $67.1 million, and this shiny new building debuted in the summer of 1997.

What makes a visit to Monona Terrace worthwhile to Wright fans is so much more than the structure itself. The gift shop sells a variety of Wright-themed trinkets, from socks to books, and one long hallway is devoted to displaying large-format photos taken by Pedro E. Guerrero, an architectural photographer hired by Wright to document his work. While you can certainly take a self-guided tour, the guided version is recommended, as it points out aspects you may not spot on your own.

DRIFTLESS AREA

Spring Valley Inn, Spring Green
Tour info: Open for overnight stays and drinks at Pat's Lounge between mid-May and early November.

If, while driving on Highway C toward Spring Green, you spotted this inn's long, cantilevered, Cherokee Red roof and spire, you wouldn't be the first to assume Wright designed it. At the entrance, the inn's name is depicted in Arts and Crafts–style lettering, and a water feature frames the reception area. Water features are a common theme in Wright's designs, from the magnificent Fallingwater in Pennsylvania, where the Kaufmanns' home was built over—not merely surrounding—a waterfall, to the mirror-like pool in front of the Annunciation Greek Orthodox Church in Wauwatosa. Wright's only college design—Florida Southern College in Lakeland, Florida—also flaunts a water feature at the heart of the campus.

The story about how this thirty-five-room inn came to be is quite the tale.

During the late 1980s, inspired by many family vacations to the area, John and Patricia Rasmussen snapped up a foreclosed building on the 10-acre wooded prairie site and plotted out a plan to build a motel to entice Taliesin visitors. Naturally, they chose Taliesin Associated Architects, overseen by Charles Montooth, a Wright apprentice. Construction began in 1991, and the inn opened in 1993.

Cole and Brenner Rasmussen are now the owners, continuing their father's legacy.

Furnishings were designed by Taliesin architect James Pfefferkorn and crafted by Rick Kraemer, a local craftsman. For example, vintage posters of Wright's sites or exhibits at museums are framed and hung in each room. Lighting and sconces were also Wright-inspired.

The building that's now Pat's Lounge—serving Wisconsin craft beer plus cocktails and wine—dates back to 1986, although the structure was not an inn at that time. It was a visitor center. Nor had it been touched by Taliesin architects. Entering the space is nearly a spiritual experience you don't always find at a bar. From the inside, the spire on the roof translates to a grand ceiling. Peach-hued sofas surround a floor-to-ceiling brick fireplace.

But even before this, the site held a deep connection to Frank Lloyd Wright. Willard Keland, the son-in-law of third-generation SC Johnson president H. F. Johnson Jr., commissioned a home by Wright in Racine, Wisconsin, during the 1950s, and was the owner of the future inn's site. As head of the Wisconsin River Development Corporation, Keland also spearheaded the purchase of 2,400 acres in 1965 to complete the construction of Taliesin's restaurant, Riverview Terrace, and what is now Taliesin's visitor center. William Wesley Peters, a Wright apprentice at Taliesin, oversaw its design.

For guests at Spring Valley Inn, a hot breakfast buffet is included in the rates. There is also an indoor pool as well as a fitness room, along with a whirlpool, steam room, and sauna. When the weather's warm, guests gather outside around the stone firepit, drinks in hand. The inn also caters to groups through its conference center, where weddings and parties are also hosted.

Although this little inn is only open from May through November, guests visit it from all over the world. "There's definitely an international presence," says Cole Rasmussen. "This morning we had a couple from Germany who flew into Chicago [to visit Taliesin]—their lifelong dream."

Taliesin, Spring Green

Tour info: There are five tours offered between May and October: 4-Hour Estate Tour, 2-Hour Highlights Tour, 2-Hour House Tour, 1-Hour House Tour, and Driftless Landscape Tour (each with their own fee). Online reservations are necessary. Taliesin also hosts photography and plein-air workshops as well as guided hikes (fee applies).

Many well-known creatives are linked to a sprawling estate now open to visitors, to help people understand who they were, and what inspired them. In Key West, Florida, the descendants of Ernest Hemingway's polydactyl cats roam his homestead, while you can step into Jackson Pollock and Lee Krasner's artistic oasis—including their 1879 home and studio—in East Hampton, New York. Similarly, painter Georgia O'Keefe's Abiquiu, New Mexico, adobe-style home contains signs of life (such as her massive collection of coffee percolators), even though she died in 1986.

In Spring Green, the sprawling 800-acre estate Frank Lloyd Wright called home beginning in 1911 is the best chance there is to get a glimpse into Wright's personality. It's recommended to take at least half a day to explore the estate, not only on a guided tour, but also to browse the gift shop (hosting the Midwest's best collection of books about Wright and decorative arts featuring his designs, from scarves to socks) and dine at the restaurant.

Wright was born in 1867 in nearby Richland Center, into a family of Unitarians of Welsh descent. His grandparents arrived from Wales during the 1840s, picking this part of Wisconsin for its rolling hills because it reminded them of their home country. This tight-knit family was also a huge presence in the region. His father was a minister and helped found the First Unitarian Society of Madison. His two progressive aunts, Jane and Nell, were teachers and ran a boarding school on the property. (Wright later designed them a new school at Taliesin, called Hillside Home School.) Wright spent many summers on his uncle's farm in Spring Green, which is now the Taliesin estate. In Welsh, *Taliesin* means shining brow, and

that's exactly what this estate looks like as it gleams under the sun, with its horizontal lines everywhere you turn.

Taliesin represents a laboratory of sorts, a place where Wright could test out his ideas, but not at the expense of the client. He also wasn't wedded to using expensive materials on these pilot projects. "He saw this as a sketch pad and called it a living laboratory where he could try out new ideas," says Roann, a guide on a recent Taliesin tour. One example is with his daughter's room, where Wright applied the concept of "human scale." The doorway and stairs are just to her size—not an adult's.

In 1932, during a point in his career when he was being lambasted for having an extramarital affair and overcharging clients, he developed the idea of the Taliesin Fellowship. Architectural students from around the country traveled to Spring Green to learn from Wright himself, living and dining on the property. Of course, following the stock market crash of 1929, there were fewer clients able to commission homes. As a result, these budding architects were forced to adopt an organic lifestyle that consisted of cooking, cleaning, farming, and helping with maintenance on the property. Thankfully, this was a brief period, and the school somewhat revived as The School of Architecture. Unfortunately, due to decisions made by the Frank Lloyd Wright Foundation, the school closed in 2020.

On a tour, you can walk through the 37,000-square-foot main house. (Square footage includes exterior spires.) Wright's Drafting Studio is also included, and represents so much square footage and inherent beauty, it's easy to see why Wright and the apprentices were so prolific here. A painting of Anna, Wright's mother, hangs above the fireplace, and a folding screen from Japan is featured on one wall. You can also see the dining room that overlooks the theater, where frequent performances—performed by apprentices on Saturdays—were often held.

Taliesin is also a testament to what the father of organic architecture had in mind, which is to not disrupt the land. "Whenever he builds something, he doesn't want to bring in a bulldozer," says Roann. "He wants the building itself to adapt." He even went so far as to harvest wood off the land and stones from local quarries. Another difference in Wright's architecture is that he appreciated aesthetics more than he did practical aspects of the design. "The way something looked superseded how it functioned," says Roann, mentioning a leaky roof, which leads to a chorus of laughter for those on the tour who know this is a common quirk in Wright's designs today.

A walk through the estate, no matter which tour you choose, provides deep insight into what Wright was thinking in terms of architecture for his own home. He loved to play piano, and so, in the main house, there's ample space for a Beckstein in the living room. Fireplaces are also in abundance, so as to cultivate family and community time. There is also an open layout in nearly all cases. "He doesn't give the rooms names," says Roann. "He just wants you to live in this open, flowing space."

Restoring the estate has not been easy. Nor has it been simple. The primary bedroom in the main house, where Frank and Olgivanna slept, for example, has undergone numerous structural changes, said another guide on a recent tour. Olgivanna's room was also renovated after Wright died, taking care not to alter, but only strengthen and support, the design—although a decision was made to remove the shag carpeting added during the 1970s. Each

room is like a piece of jewelry in a jewelry box, sporting its own identity, but also adopting cohesion. For example, the Garden Room is the room in the house with the most Southwestern art, Asian art is everywhere, and the original blue lounge chairs bought at Marshall Field's are still in the loggia.

Even though Wright died in 1959, there is at least one person on the estate who remembers living and working alongside him. Minerva Montooth, who turned ninety-eight in 2022, resides in an apartment tucked away near the main house. She can't imagine living anywhere else. "People ask me, 'When did [you] come?' and I say 'Year one.'" She adds that this place has felt more like home than anywhere else she's lived. "I'm living in a work of art."

Since 1947 she's been associated with the estate's Taliesin Fellowship, after moving here with her late husband, architect Charles Montooth, and her twin sister, who was married to Taliesin's farm manager. Wright used to joke with the twins that they looked too much alike, and, to Minerva, said, "You should change something so I can recognize you."

"I didn't know a thing about architecture, and still don't," quips Montooth.

Wright even hosted their 1952 wedding at Taliesin West. Minerva's commitments to Taliesin include planning programming and special events on behalf of the Fellowship, as well as advising apprentices and reviewing their applications. While she currently lives in the apartment where her sister lived, before that she lived with her husband in another structure, next to the chicken coops. Wright apprentice William Wesley Peters lived in the apartment

before Montooth's sister did. "It's quiet here. Too quiet. I'm used to the apprentices coming in," says Montooth.

Minerva was Olgivanna's personal assistant from 1962 to 1985. Once, she had Frank and Olgivanna over for lunch, serving veal in cream sauce. "Mrs. Wright said, 'It was very rich for his diet,'" recalls Montooth. "She had an iron fist. She was a wonderful person. She was very laid-back, too." She points to a framed black-and-white photo of Mr. and Mrs. Wright in the apartment's living room. "She was beautiful and lovely," recalls Montooth. "She didn't want to take any credit or glory away from [Mr. Wright]."

A. D. German Warehouse, Richland Center

Tour info: Guided tour price includes a short film and are offered at 11:15 a.m., 12:15 p.m., 1:15 p.m., and 2:15 p.m. Private tours are also available for a higher fee. Call ahead (600-647-1715) to book. adgermanwarehouse.org

As the only Wright-designed structure in the city of his birth, and the only warehouse he designed, A. D. German Warehouse was built between 1917 and 1921. The idea was to give merchant Albert Dell German additional storage space for his wholesale business, stocking groceries and pantry staples like flour, sugar, tobacco, grains, and feed. Like Wright, German had Welsh roots. German emigrated to the United States with his parents from Wales, and later to Richland County, home to Richland Center.

"He was a little ahead of his time, [so it] makes sense he would have a building designed by Frank Lloyd Wright," says Derek Kalish, the A. D. German Warehouse Conservancy's president.

For the four-floor, 20,000-square-foot concrete building, adjacent to a warehouse German already owned, Wright opted for a Mayan Revival architectural style. Warehouse purchases were delivered in the community by horse and buggy.

Wright scholars strongly feel his work at that time on such major projects as the Imperial Hotel in Tokyo and the Larkin Building in Buffalo, New York—neither of which are still standing—influenced the warehouse design. In fact, the A. D. German Warehouse is a significant structure because it's the only remaining commercial building Wright designed during this time period. There are also similarities to the Frederick C. Bogk House in Milwaukee. They each boast exterior brick and, on top, concrete friezes with cast-concrete ornamental art. There are also associations with Wright's Mayan Temple admiration, seen in Hollyhock House and the Harriett and Samuel Freeman House, both in Los Angeles.

Construction of this poured-concrete-style building came to a halt in 1921 after four years of work. Wright had initially quoted $30,000. The building ultimately cost $125,000. Followers of Wright's work should not be surprised, as every one of his projects came in way over budget. It's also thought that Wright built the warehouse to pay off a debt to German for supplies purchased there while building Taliesin. German continued to use the warehouse for its intended use, however, despite the design work not being fully realized. During the late 1930s, German left town. It sat empty for a long while.

In 1974 the building earned a spot on the National Register of Historic Places. Involving benefactors and members of the local community in fund-raising has been key over the years. Numerous grants along with state and federal historic tax credits help to power this ongoing effort. In exchange for a donation, one can purchase a custom-engraved paver, in memory of a loved one, or depicting the name of a business proud to support the restoration.

Since 2013, the warehouse and adjacent site have been managed and owned by the Conservancy, after Glenn Schnadt bought the property and gifted it to the organization. The Conservancy is in the beginning stages of a full-on restoration that, once complete, will usher in a new chapter. Plans are to use the building as a mixed-use venue: for venues, retail, heritage tourism, educational outreach, and cultural programming.

But first, the rooms had to be cleared out. "The place was full," recalls Kalish. "The person who had it before collected everything under the sun."

Recent renovations include the roof, drainage projects, windows, and heating components. Because it was designed to be a cold-storage building, heating needed to be added, ensuring it was up to code. Open shelving along one wall added by Jack Howe, a Wright apprentice, has been removed. The Conservancy is working with Isthmus Architecture, a preservation architecture firm in Madison, to fully realize the warehouse's next chapter: a community hub with space for entrepreneurs, shops, and restaurants, along with event space. Each of the five floors boasts 4,000 square feet.

On the ground floor, the open layout will be inviting.

"This will be a venue space," says Kalish, on a tour outlining the upcoming work needed at the warehouse, and what it will look like when complete. "The basement will have a cheese-aging cave and facility for around nine or ten people." This might sound like an odd addition to a multipurpose building, but this is the heart of cheese country, after all. Just down the road, two cheese retailers have won big at the World Championship Cheese Contest: Carr Valley Cheese Co.'s Mazomanie store (the creamery is in La Valle) and Arena Cheese in Arena. This part of Wisconsin is in desperate need of spots to age cheese, says Kalish.

Richland Center's dwindling population has created a need for new reasons to retain its residents. According to Kalish, the population declined from 6,000 to 5,000 in the last census.

"This building has to give back to the community in some way, shape, or form," he says. "I want to see the building utilized by the community." One example might be the offices of a mental-health organization. "That's a sector not served by rural communities," he says, citing a lack of funding in the county and a shortage of counselors. In past years, a haunted house was hosted in the warehouse, creating frightful delights that Wright might never have intended, but a bonding opportunity for the community, all the same. nonetheless. Visitors flock from all over the world to see this building under construction and ask county officials, including Kalish, for a tour.

"We're still learning as we go," says Kalish. "This is like a living project. There's value in restoring old buildings. They're part of a community's fabric."

Wyoming Valley School Cultural Arts Center, Wyoming Spring Green

Tour info: Tours offered Wednesday–Saturday, 11 a.m., 1 p.m., and 2 p.m., between mid-June and mid-September (fee applies). wyomingvalleyschool.org

While this elementary school on 2 pastoral acres represents the only time that Wright was commissioned to design a Wisconsin school, he'd actually already added a school to his design portfolio. The Hillside School was built in 1902 at nearby Taliesin, where he grew up and spent his adult years in Spring Green, for his two aunts, who were teachers.

With its flat roof and clerestory windows, this school was established on land partially donated by Wright, who also donated his design services. It was built in 1957 as a means to consolidate six one-room schoolhouses, and in 1958 welcomed its first class of forty-eight students, between the first and eighth grades.

After being dormant since 1990, the concrete-block structure reopened in 2011 as a cultural arts center. It boasts a robust calendar of art shows and is also bookable for private events, garnering additional revenue for restoration efforts.

In 2021 Dave Zaleski was hired as executive director, after working at Taliesin and the Racine Art Museum in Racine. He's tasked with handling private rentals—for weddings and business retreats—while also creating awareness of this lesser-known Wright project. Many visit Taliesin and have no idea this school even exists, or that you can tour it. In some ways, it mirrors the separation between Wright and Spring Green around the time this school was designed and built.

"Spring Green and Wright never had a good relationship," says Zaleski. "Surprisingly, the school district asked Wright to design this."

Wright's experience of being raised by three educators—his mom and his two aunts—meant he knew what an ideal educational environment should look like. Placing the school back from the highway and built into the hillside became a priority for him, which is what inspired him to donate part of the land to make this happen. Next, he added his own imprint, borrowing inspiration from the many homes he'd designed. There are two fireplaces and his signature red flooring.

Like many Wright projects, the quoted price changed. Quoted at $40,000, it came in $2,000 over budget. Marshall Erdman, owner of Marshall Erdman & Associates, a construction company, ended up saving him. He covered some of the cost overruns. Wright and Erdman had already worked together on the First Unitarian Society Meeting House in Madison as well as prefab homes around the state (including the Joseph Mollica House in Bayside).

With just two classrooms, the two teachers switched between classes so as not to disrupt the students. Older kids were taught to mentor the younger kids. In 1977 the school's population changed to accommodate only fourth graders for the district's "Year in the Country" programming, geared for that grade level.

Restoring the structure has meant renovating all systems, jacking up a portion of the foundation (because it had settled over time), refinishing mahogany sheeting over Douglas pine wood beams, and installing a new ceiling (due to roof damage). Mahogany vent doors were made from scratch in the spirit of the originals, working from photos. A new chimney and air-conditioning were added. And the acoustics in the former lunchroom were upgraded to accommodate musical performances.

"Wright was historically a horrible engineer, and fortunately we did not have structural issues," says Zaleski. Concrete block had been painted yellow, which is now back to gray. Mouse droppings were everywhere. Windowsills were rotted and bore wide gaps. "It was raining Asian beetles. When I started, I cleaned for three weeks," he recalls, and wore a respirator while doing so.

The Wisconsin Economic Development Corporation awarded them a grant to assist with these efforts, and Peter Rott with Isthmus Architecture created the new designs.

"It basically sat for twenty years," says Zaleski. "People bought it, but they didn't know what to do with it"—until a benefactor came along with a vision and the funds. Working with Gerald Opgenorth, a local attorney, they formed the Wyoming Valley School, Inc., which functions as a nonprofit. Opgenorth served as its first president.

Former students and teachers have dropped in over the years to help fill in the gaps of how this school functioned. "Bob remembers every single detail," says Zaleski, about a former

student. "He's been a huge help." Another benefit has been old photos, showing how the rooms were used and their furnishings arranged. While those original desks and chairs are now gone, new ones in their place help visitors imagine a day in the life at this school.

Hosting weddings, events, performances and art shows also brings the building back to its roots.

In the 1970s, the school hosted Lumberjack Days as a class activity, where kids dressed up as lumberjacks served the adults pancakes.

During the summer of 2021, the Wyoming Valley School Cultural Arts Center hosted a wedding, for a couple now living in New York City who both work in fine-art and fashion photography and whose photos have appeared in *Vogue*. They invited around a hundred guests. "Everyone was wearing couture," says Zaleski about the couple. For example, the groom wore a 1960s tweed suit.

Could this become Spring Green's hottest wedding venue? Zaleski is banking on that. After all, this schoolhouse has been all about innovation—including the day the first class of students moved in.

"They went from *Little House on the Prairie* to this," says Zaleski, gesturing around to one of Wright's masterpieces. "Think about it."

TWO RIVERS

Bernard and Fern Schwartz House ("Still Bend"), Two Rivers

Tour info: Open for overnight stays with a two-night minimum. Hour-long tours on select dates are posted on the website (fee applies) and reservations are required. stillbend.com

Entering this 3,000-square-foot, two-story Usonian—also referred to as "Still Bend"—is akin to dialing it back to the 1940s. Owners Michael and Gary Ditmer have decorated every nook and cranny with relics from this Midcentury Modern time period—right on down to the glassware stocked on the bar cart. It's fitting, as the home was completed in the spring of 1940, for local businessman Bernard Schwartz and his wife, Fern. "What we're trying to do is get out any visual cues that are past 1969," says Michael Ditmer, who with his brother is the home's third set of owners. "It's a time-travel machine for the 1940s through the 1960s. I'm not going to bring in a brown toaster oven with little flowers on it."

The Ditmers bought this house in 2003 and quickly embarked on major restorations. The house was covered in siding, hiding Wright's original design of cypress boards. Exterior brick was spalling badly. The balcony off one bedroom had been infested with carpenter ants, and the roof was leaking, too, resulting in water stains on the ceilings. French doors and other exterior doors were replaced with plate-glass windows. The kitchen was last remodeled in the 1970s.

A year later they were ready to rent it out for overnight stays, giving guests an opportunity to experience what it's like to live in a Wright home.

"At that time, the only other Frank Lloyd Wright place [where] you could stay the night was the Seth Peterson Cottage," says Michael Ditmer. "We're not a house museum. We call it a living-house museum." Rates range from $595 to $795 per night, with a two-night minimum. "The whole thing, from the beginning, was to crowdsource the restoration," he says. "All the money we bring in [from tours and overnight rentals] goes right back into the house."

It's crucial that people experience the house in order to garner support for this ongoing restoration—both financial and emotional. Next up, a wall of windows installed during the 1970s will be removed in favor of Wright's original design: French doors. Another upcoming project is fulfilling Wright's landscaping plans for this site. "It's hard to put it into words, what it is. Everyone has their own experience, but it's a calming experience usually," says Michael about the lucky ones who get to stay in this house. "We have people come back every year now, and from twenty-eight different countries."

Removing the siding to reveal the red brick beneath was one immediate task after buying the home. Then came a desire to fill in the house's history as much as possible. Michael invited Wright apprentice Edgar Tafel to the home and hosted an interview with him in the living room, in an attempt to understand Wright's intention with building this home. "It's a project

we wanted to do—to build it the way Wright intended," says Michael, also referring to the sunken garden in the original design, which has since been realized by the Ditmers. "It always comes back to what Wright intended, and I always go to what Wright would think."

Ditmer's first introduction to Wright came as a child. "My parents had taken me to Taliesin when I was sixteen years old. I couldn't tour it yet, but I walked the grounds. I think that first started my interest in Frank Lloyd Wright," he says.

The Schwartzes lived in the home until 1971 and raised their son Steven here. Steven, who is now in his eighties, maintains contact with the Ditmers to share his stories of growing up in the home. "He's been important [when it comes] to telling us things that were not in the drawings," says Jenny Lee, a frequent tour guide of the home. After the Schwartzes, a couple with five children moved in and resided here for thirty-three years.

For a *Life* issue in 1938, prototype homes were featured, including this one of Wright's. When the Schwartzes saw the article, they vowed to have that exact home built. Bernard placed a call to Wright. "At that time," says Lee, "he was on an upswing, being on the cover of *Time*." The design was altered slightly for the exterior, swapping out the stone and stucco for red tidewater cypress board and batten, along with red brick. "There was a lot more articulation," explains Michael Ditmer, "of the ceiling heights in the built design," specifically, a balcony overlooking the living room, not in the *Life* design. Wright also designed beds, chairs, tables, lamps, a couch with built-in bookshelves, bathroom cabinets, and even wastebaskets and fruit bowls to complete the home's interior.

Ditmer explains the philosophy behind this *Life* design best. "The whole idea was to find out if people wanted to live in modern houses or stick with traditional," he says.

Bernard was known to have fancied Wright, maybe even idolized him, much to Fern's dismay. "He had a man crush on Wright and would walk around town with a cape and hat, [fancying] himself to be like Wright," says Ditmer. Fern, however, was into Victorian-era interior design.

Before this home was built along a river that feeds into Lake Michigan, the neighborhood was entirely rural. No other homes had been built. "The aerial photography shows a red barn off that way," says Lee, gesturing beyond the home, but that was it.

Wright used red cypress for interior walls, including the ceiling, and red bricks were chosen for the exterior. A mezzanine overlooking the second floor makes the home feel entirely open, yet also creates privacy for the three upstairs bedrooms. Within the clerestory windows are cutouts unique to this home. Built-ins are in abundance in the living room, as are built-in banquette seating. Three fireplaces anchor the living room, and one in the sunken exterior court. One claim to fame here is that this house is believed to boast the longest continuously running radiant floor heating in the United States. It is only the fifth Usonian to feature this type of heating. Similar to other Usonians, concrete square floor tiles mark the first floor's flooring, but in this case, they are much larger, each one measuring as a 7-foot square module. About 7 feet by 7 feet. Instead of Pyrex-glass tubes, part of the *Life* design, as a light source, a band of clerestory windows became part of the Schwartz House design. "That whole scheme of the Pyrex tubes was bouncing around in Wright's head, but he had never put it in a house," says Ditmer.

The primary suite is a sunken space off the entry with an en suite bath. This suite also leads to a new sunken room the Dinners installed, based on Wright's original design. Except for 1957 Kohler robin's-egg-blue fixtures installed in the powder room off the entry in 2018, the other three baths feature late-1930s fixtures installed at the time the home was built.

At night, from the back of the house, it looks like a Chinese lantern—due to the landscape lighting, of course, but also Wright's clean lines.

"It's timeless," says Lee. "This house could have been built this year. I really do feel a primal essence of Wright. He's going to control you from the moment you walk into this home." This includes the long entry's compression-and-release design technique. Another defining feature is the acoustics. Sitting in a chair and strumming a guitar, you'll find that it never sounded so good.

"It was really meant for having people," says Lee. "People can stay here just like they were living here."

It's a rare Wright home in that it's open for overnight rentals—if you can snag a reservation, that is. After appearing on the Netflix show *The World's Most Amazing Vacation Rentals*, the calendar is booked out for nearly a year with a two-night minimum.

Tour dates are published on the home's website, the dates coinciding with when the home is not rented out. On a recent tour, Lee took a mix of locals and traveling architecture fans through the home. While her admiration for Wright is apparent now, she actually knew about Wright from a very young age. "Fallingwater was the first [Wright-designed home I visited]," she says. "My father took us there on a vacation. That never left my brain—that you could live in nature."

FOX CITIES

Stephen M. B. Hunt II House, Oshkosh

Tour info: This is a private residence and not open for tours. Please respect the owners' privacy.

As new empty nesters, Kelly Radandt and Scott Huiras were ready to move, but didn't want to leave the block. They loved the unique, historical homes in the Algoma Boulevard Historic District.

"We lived for twenty years in a [Queen Anne] Victorian home five houses up," says Radandt. "As we're aging, we thought it would be nice to have a little home." They took the plunge and asked Harold Buchholz, then-owner of the creamy-white Stephen M. B. Hunt II House with its brown trim, down the street, if he'd like to sell—to them. Their timing was good. After twenty-three years in the home, Buchholz yearned to travel more. The trio worked

out a deal where Buchholz sold them the two-bedroom, two-bath Prairie-style stucco house, and he paid them rent until he was ready to depart.

The couple downsized from the larger house in preparation for moving in. The home features key tenets of Wright's designs, such as built-in shelves throughout the home and on each side of the brick fireplace, original stained-glass windows, and sconces resembling small wood boxes. A wall of built-in storage marks one of the bedrooms. Above the dining-room table they hung a custom-made Craftsman-style light fixture featuring wood and stained glass. Visits to Taliesin in Spring Green and Taliesin West in Scottsdale, Arizona, have further coached them on living in a Wright-designed home.

"He actually passed away in this home," says Radandt about the owner before them, "which is very special to us." A framed photo of Buchholz sits proudly on a bookshelf in the living room for all who enter to see, "as we had promised him we'd do."

Buchholz worshipped Wright's designs. What drew him to Oshkosh was news of the home being on the market. He'd always wanted to live in a Wright-designed home. "He had, like, two hundred Frank Lloyd Wright books when he died," says Radandt.

The couple embarked on eight months of overdue restorations to the 1917 home—built for Stephen Hunt, vice president of McMillen Lumber Co., as his second Wright-designed home—that included building a new garage, remodeling the kitchen, replastering the walls, finishing the floors, and applying fresh coats of paint inside and out. The primary bedroom was also updated, and so was the bath, with the original wood medicine cabinet retained. Having the original plans has been a godsend. "We're trying to get it back [to what it was]," says Radandt.

This is Wright's only Oshkosh structure. But he did build a second home for Hunt, in La Grange, Illinois, referred to as the Steven M. B. Hunt II House. Designed in 1907, it was one of four homes Wright designed in the suburb west of Chicago.

Cathy Huber, their good friend, is a former local prosecutor and lists genealogy as a hobby. She embarked on a lengthy research project about the home's provenance before the couple moved in. "I took the house as a person, as it were," she says, and consulted Ancestry.com, census records, and the local paper.

Hunt grew up in a large Chicago-area family and was influential in the Oshkosh community, along with his wife, who sat on the school board. Until one day, he took out an ad in the paper declaring that he was leaving town and selling the house. They abruptly moved to Kansas City in 1920. It was later bought by Max Silver, of Polish-Jewish descent, who skimmed from private Chicago banks he'd owned with his brother. He ran off with a mistress to Canada to avoid prosecution, and his brother, Adolph, became the subject of a national manhunt, before coming back of his own accord. Max resurfaced in California, where he'd moved with his kids and wife, remarrying the wealthy owner of a clothing-store chain after his wife died and becoming "the toast of the town," says Huber, featured prominently in society pages. The next owner, Isadore Meyer Block, owned a scrap-metal business and lived with his family in

the house from 1924 until the late 1940s. His son became a folk-music singer in New York City and acquainted with Bob Dylan. There were a few more owners before Buchholz came along.

Despite all of the restoration work as the current stewards of the home, the couple never forgot Buchholz's parting words after they finalized the sale. "He said, 'You're going to fall in love with this home,'" says Radandt. "This house just has a real Zen feeling to it."

CENTRAL WISCONSIN

E. Clarke and Julia Arnold House, Columbus
Tour info: This is a private residence and not open for tours. Please respect the owners' privacy.

When Mary Arnold swings open the door to her Usonian-style home, she immediately shares how she feels about it. "This is our house. We live here. This is not a museum," she says, standing in the entry.

Indeed, the word *cozy* comes to mind as you walk through the rooms, particularly the living room with Wright's classic built-in banquette seating and radiant floor heating. Sandstone quarried in Sauk City comprises the walls. Each overhang was reinforced with steel at the hands of William Wesley Peters.

Arnold, who served as the mayor of her town of around 5,300 residents at the time this book was written, is an unusual owner of a Frank Lloyd Wright–designed home. Not only is this where she and her husband live—and raised their two children—but she grew up here, too. Arnold and her parents are the only people to have owned the home since it was built in 1954. The family moved out of a rambling Victorian, also in Columbus. "It was all alfalfa fields," recalls Arnold on move-in day. Over time, more homes were built, creating a neighborhood. It was because her parents' good friends, Patrick and Margaret Kinney, had

commissioned Wright to build them a Usonian in Lancaster, in 1951, that they even considered building this one.

"My dad was understated. He had a very dry sense of humor," says Arnold, and attracted to Ru's very opposite demeanor. "Ru was this big, loud Irishman." The second generation of these two families still keeps in touch. Also, Archie Kinney, the Kinneys' grand-nephew, studied at Taliesin's School of Architecture just before it shut down in 2021, no doubt inspired by his time in their home.

Arnold was seven years old and in the second grade when her parents bought the house. Three years later, at the age of forty, her mother gave birth to twins. This lifestyle change necessitated a few tweaks to the home's design, including installing carpeting to protect the twins' rough-and-tumble play. In 1959, a third wing by Wright apprentice John Howe accommodated the growing family by adding a half bath, bringing the total number to three; a den; and a bedroom, along with built-in storage along the hallway. It also changed the home's configuration to that of a "Y."

There are four bedrooms in the home. To this day, few changes have been made, in an attempt to honor Wright's original design. Although tiles and countertops in one bath were swapped out for a more modern aesthetic, original cabinetry remains. "It used to be that popular Pepto-Bismol pink," says Arnold. "I think the countertops were yellow when I was growing up."

One notable difference in this Usonian is the lack of Cherokee Red concrete flooring. "My mother did not like Cherokee Red, so she convinced [Wright] not to do it," says Arnold.

After Arnold's parents died in 2004 and 2005, she made the decision to move back into her childhood home in 2009 with her husband, Henry St. Maurice, and one of their two

children. St. Maurice didn't need convincing, as the farm that had been in his family for fifty years had been sold abruptly. "If you'd like to keep it, you really [won't] have a second chance," he told his wife.

Memories of her childhood abound even today as she takes people on a tour of the home. There are the windows the twins would climb out of in their bedroom. "And the bar would call my mom and say, 'The twins are out again!'"

The twins died young—both in their twenties, and of leukemia, although in different years—and their other sister, Margaret, passed in her twenties, too, of a rare liver disease. Keeping the home in the family is a way Arnold can continue to feel close to her siblings.

Slowly, the family made the home their own, adding a wood-burning stove and tackling updates, such as installing a new roof and air-conditioning, along with adding insulation. Whereas in the past, when Arnold was young, the family would throw open all the windows and go to the air-conditioned movie theater, this time around, they no longer wanted to do that. They also replaced the sun porch's screens with windows, plus added skylights for more natural light. "My mother would spend a lot of time out here in the summer and read," says Arnold, wistfully. Now the sunroom can be enjoyed year-round. Furnishings by local maker Robert Black—a cocktail table, stereo console, and coffee table—are also in the home. The coffee table's marble top was sourced from the former First National Bank in downtown Columbus, which was tucked inside a 1916 neoclassical building.

In many cases, these updates were necessary. "My dad was not a handyman," says Arnold. "We found a lot of things he fixed with Scotch tape." In the process of going through her parents' possessions she found a letter he wrote to Wright, thanking him for a check he donated to the Wisconsin Historical Society. "They had a very cordial relationship," says Arnold. It's now

framed and hung in the home. The couple is also cataloging receipts for past home repairs, to better understand the work that's been done.

Each May, they open their home to fifth-grade students at Wakanda Elementary School in Menomonie to deepen their studies within a Wright-focused curriculum. If Wright enthusiasts happen to be taking photos from the street, they'll often invite them in. Once, a French architect arrived with his family. Arnold and St. Maurice later visited them during a Paris trip. Another time, St. Maurice was mowing the lawn when a couple from Australia came up to him. They wanted to see the house, and he let them in. The home features many original design elements, such as covers on the living room's banquette cushions and a Formica built-in in what used to be Arnold's older sister's bedroom, then the twins' bedroom, and is now an office. In 2001 Arnold's parents updated the kitchen slightly. Despite this being Wright's design, E. Clarke was successful in putting his imprint on the family home. "He had been encouraged by staff not to present ideas directly to Mr Wright but he did it anyway and got what he wanted," says Arnold.

One example was moving the wings farther away from their axis, thus creating a better view of the yard through the kitchen and living room's walls of windows. "My dad wanted to see the sunset," says Arnold. "They really are gorgeous out here."

Field's at the Wilderness, Wisconsin Dells
Tour info: Open for dining daily from 4 p.m. (bar) and 4:30 p.m. (restaurant).
fieldsatthewilderness.com

Many who walk into this restaurant mistake it for a former church. And no wonder. There's a vaulted ceiling with stained-glass windows. But if you look deeper, it's an architectural marvel that just happens to serve amazing food, with an open kitchen, exposed-brick walls, a water feature, and wooden carts containing food orders that are wheeled to each table.

Open since 2000 and based on Wright protégé James Dresser's design, the restaurant was founded by two brothers, Robert and Tim Field. Five years ago, Wilderness Resort took over the ownership when the Fields retired. (Upon arrival, if you look to your left, a water slide literally protrudes from a resort building like an elbow.)

But even before that, Field's was a well-known name among foodies in Central Wisconsin. The original Field's (Field's Steak & Stein) was a hopping restaurant just north of the Dells. In its early days, waiters at Field's at the Wilderness wore tuxedos and diners dressed to the nines to dine on surf and turf.

Just like at The Del-Bar, a supper-club-style restaurant in nearby Lake Delton also designed by Dresser, the decision to hire Dresser was easy; he was already a customer. Although his

portfolio spoke for itself, says general manager Ryan Hasheider, who began working at the first Field's in 1994. "Robert and Tim approached him because of his work at The Del-Bar."

This newer incarnation is a tad more casual and serves seafood, steak, and pizzas cooked in a wood-burning oven. Drinks range from the classic brandy old-fashioned to a Door County cocktail, the hints of cherries a nostalgic nod to the state's cherry-growing region. Throughout the menu are nods to local spirits.

"I dealt with him many times," recalls Hasheider. "He's an interesting fellow, a spry old fellow." Including the chairs Dresser designed, his vision is intact, including a kidney-shaped bar in the back of the restaurant that fills an entire dining room.

But despite all the fans, there's a handful of critics. "We get comments from people that it's outdated," says Hasheider, who is armed with a quick retort: "It was outdated when it was built."

Seth Peterson Cottage, Lake Delton

Tour info: Guided tours offered on the second Sunday of the month from 1:00–3:30 p.m. (fee applies). Reservations not required. Overnight stays require a two-night minimum. sethpeterson.org

From the outside, you might think this is a modern glass-walled cottage tucked into the woods along Mirror Lake in Mirror Lake State Park. All of this is true—except there's much more to the story.

Built in 1958 for a young man named Seth Peterson, it's among Wright's smallest designs, at 880 square feet. An open floor plan and walls of windows easily connect with the outdoors, no matter the season. The space consists of a kitchen, bath, and bedroom, and a living room and dining room that are seamlessly connected. Anchoring the layout is a fireplace crafted from the same buff-colored sandstone as the exterior, sourced from a quarry in nearby Rock Springs. There are only two interior doors: one leading to the bath, and the other, to the utility closet. A sloped roof at varying heights—from 6–8 feet to 12 feet—allows sun to pour into the cottage while also sheltering it from harsh rays. The cottage's high ceilings make the space feel much roomier than it actually is, a concept Wright no doubt intended. In the bedroom, a band of windows invites light in but also provides privacy.

This is considered a variation on Wright's Usonian homes, on a much smaller scale. It was also Wright's final Wisconsin commission, although his design plans for other projects,

including the Annunciation Greek Orthodox Church, had been in the works since many years prior, and were completed after his 1959 death.

Who was Seth Peterson, the young man who commissioned this cottage?

Peterson grew up in Black Earth, Wisconsin. After touring numerous Wright projects in Illinois and Wisconsin, he tried to become a Taliesin apprentice, but failed. He worked as a computer operator for the State of Wisconsin's Department of Motor Vehicles, and had been honorably discharged from the army due to his asthma. He bought this site of 1.18 acres in 1958, which included a small cottage at the time. After the cottage burned to the ground shortly thereafter, he resorted to camping on the land.

Still burned from not being accepted into the Taliesin Fellowship program, due to not having the $1,500 tuition, Peterson asked Wright to design a cottage for him and his fiancée. Surprisingly, Wright said yes. Although he never visited the site, two of his apprentices did: Tom Casey and John Howe. Another apprentice, William Wesley Peters, frequently claimed the cottage features more architecture per square foot than any other Wright-designed building.

Wright's absence didn't indicate a lack of emotional connection to this project. Using a topographic map, along with plenty of photographs, Wright selected the perfect spot to build the cottage: perched on a bluff and facing the lake sideways.

"The way it's sited is what makes it so special," says Bill Martinelli. A retired architectural draftsman from a Madison engineering firm, Martinelli's involvement with this project connects both his professional career and his personal passion for conserving architecture.

"Frank Lloyd Wright had no need to build a cottage," says Greg Kliner, a frequent tour guide during the cottage's open houses, held on the second Sunday of each month. "He was working on the Guggenheim. He didn't need to do this."

At twenty-two years old, Peterson may have also been among the youngest people to commission a design from Wright. His homes were not cheap, but this one fell into a modest price range and was not cookie-cutter, like any of the American System-Built model homes may have been when built between 1912 and 1917. This one stood out on its own, however. To save money on the overall budget, a garage was nixed, as was a basement or attic. The walls were not painted or plastered, another money-saving tactic.

Peterson died by his own hand before the cottage was fully completed. His engagement with his fiancée had ended, and he was experiencing financial hurdles in paying off the cottage. It all proved to be too much for Peterson, and he took his own life in April 1960.

Owen Pritchard lived here from 1962 to 1966. He raised Afghan hounds, and later sold the cottage to the State of Wisconsin, for inclusion in the new Mirror Lake State Park.

It was unoccupied until 1992, boarded up all those years once state officials, as well as members of the Mirror Lake Association, realized its architectural pedigree.

As is the case when a house is abandoned, it led to derelict conditions. The roof was rotting, water had infiltrated the ceiling, and the plumbing, electrical, and mechanicals needed replacing. Restoring the cottage by new owners would take some heavy lifting.

It wasn't until Audrey Laatsch was paddling along Mirror Lake—a body of water so named for its mirror-like surface—and noticed a sweet little cottage up the hill that this cottage was rescued. In the fall of 1989, a group of about fifty people, including Laatsch, Bill

Martinelli, the Mirror Lake Association, the Department of Natural Resources, and the State Historical Society of Wisconsin, met in nearby Wisconsin Dells to plot out a path to save it, forming the Seth Peterson Cottage Conservancy.

"[Audrey] was the woman that got this whole thing started," says Martinelli of Laatsch, who died in 2002. "She was the one that pushed it through. You don't always realize until someone's gone what all they were doing.

"I grew up in the Westmoreland neighborhood," Martinelli recalls, "not too far from the Jacobs I House," he recalls. "I was interested in architecture ever since I was a kid. I've been to every Wright building in the United States."

Architect John Eifler, who by then had worked on many Wright projects, offered his services to restore this home back to what it should have been. During the restoration, which cost around $350,000, everything but the masonry was addressed. Furnishings designed by Wright, but never built, were finally constructed. Wright-like furnishings, including two plywood chairs facing the fireplace, were designed by architect Eifler.

"We had all the furniture built as part of the restoration," says Martinelli. Built-in banquette seating was also built according to Wright's plans. Radiant floor heating, expensive in 1958, but part of the original design, was finally added. In order to do this, each large, heavy rock in the flagstone flooring had to be removed and reassembled, a huge undertaking. Volunteers numbered each rock before it was placed back into the floor. The Andy Warhol

Foundation was among the donors to help finance the restoration. Pella Windows & Doors donated custom windows, and Kohler, a Wisconsin plumbing manufacturer, donated fixtures similar to Wright's intended "desert sand" hue.

Two other important people were part of the process: Seth Peterson's sister, Carolyn Royster; and his close friend, Bert Goderstad. They helped guide the team with their anecdotes and letters about Peterson's intended use of the cottage.

When the cottage was first built, the area was not yet in Mirror Lake State Park. And even if it had been, Wisconsin state parks did not host overnight structures like they do today. Your only option was to pitch a tent. When this cottage hosted its first overnight guests in 1992—as both a source of revenue to fund the restoration, and a way to introduce people to Wright's designs—it was the only Wright-designed structure in the country where you could stay overnight.

"What better way for people to learn about Frank Lloyd Wright than to stay here? That was genius on her part," says Martinelli, referring to Audrey's commitment to restore this cottage. "We have a good group of volunteers that come up every year [to thoroughly clean and maintain the property during our spring work week]."

On many days, whether it's snowing, rainy, or sunny, the only sound you can hear is that of birds chirping—thanks not only to the forested surroundings, but a bird feeder in full view of the home's wall of windows in the living room. If it's a nice day, the terrace overlooking the lake is wide enough to practice yoga or eat dinner outdoors. A canoe tied up on the cottage's dock down the hill encourages guests to further explore the area, discovering for themselves what Peterson found so magical about this little spot.

"Seth's name lives on now," says Martinelli. "His name is now associated with a piece of famous architecture."

The Del-Bar, Wisconsin Dells
Tour info: Restaurant and bar open daily from 4 p.m. to 9 p.m. del-bar.com

As the story goes, the design for this supper club was born out of a napkin drawing by frequent diner James Dresser, a protégé of Wright's.

"In 1948 James Dresser started coming into The Del-Bar. [He] told my grandpa he had some ideas [about] how to expand, and wanted to do some drawings for him," says Amy Wimmer, its third-generation owner. She and her sister, Anne Stoken, took over from their father and stepmother in 2018.

At the time, the supper club ran out of a 1938 log cabin. Wimmer's grandparents were the second owners and purchased it in 1943. Dresser dreamt up a design with low ceilings and five dining rooms, two of them sunken, plus an indoor terrace. One dining room overlooks a koi pond. Another has vaulted ceilings. There is also an outdoor patio. "No matter where you sit, every table has a fantastic view," says Jane Wimmer, a second-generation owner.

Few changes have been made, and those are more about safety than design. This includes removing flagstone steps in the bar. "People would have too many cocktails and head to the dining room," says Wimmer. "They were twisting their ankles. My grandpa said [to Dresser], 'You've got to fill this floor in.'" Another recent design update was in the women's restroom,

which hadn't been renovated in thirty years. "We tried to leave it a little retro, but also freshen it up," says Wimmer. "We really take our time on renovations in order to keep it fresh."

Five years ago, Wimmer moved back home from Colorado to take over The Del-Bar. She did not change the name, and tweaked the menu only slightly. She's continually got an eye on offering a high-end dining experience while still honoring the supper-club tradition. "You make your reservations, have some time at the bar, sit down to dinner, and have an ice-cream drink at the bar after," she says about a typical night at a supper club.

Working with local farmers and food suppliers is important to Wimmer. "Everything we can get local, we do," she says. This includes Hidden Valley Mushroom Farm and Country Pumpkin Farm Market, both in Wisconsin Dells. Neesvig's steaks are sourced from the Madison area. "All of our cheese comes from Carr Valley, and our cheese curds from Sassy Cow Creamery." Salads switch up often to reflect what's fresh and in season.

The same chef has worked the grills for thirty years. "We've had servers who have been with us for twenty or thirty years," says Wimmer. "They get requests [from diners] all the time."

Vivid artwork—a mix of landscapes and food-related still-lifes, by Mary Alice Cullen Wimmer, who is Amy's aunt—hangs on the walls of the lobby and in the Copper Room.

Canoe Bay, Chetek

Tour info: Open for overnight stays daily; restaurant open to hotel guests only. canoebay.com

On the grounds of a former church camp—one he himself attended as a young boy, adjacent to land his grandfather owned—Dan Dobrowolski realized his dream of a design-driven luxury resort. In 1993 he opened Canoe Bay with his wife, Lisa. The resort is just outside of a small town of around 2,200 people, just south of Rice Lake, a drive of just 2 hours and 15 minutes from the Twin Cities.

Thankfully, Dobrowolski already knew a good architect: John Rattenbury, a protégé of Wright's who ran Taliesin Architects. Rattenbury partnered with Wright on the Marin County Civic Center in Northern California and the Guggenheim Museum in New York City. He also designed the King Kamehameha Golf Club in Maui, Hawaii. Rattenbury died in 2021 at the age of ninety-two.

Rattenbury designed two of the cabins on the property. Although all Canoe Bay cabins are luxurious, Rattenbury's are the most luxurious and command the highest nightly rate. The Rattenbury cottage opened in 1999, and the other, Edgewood, in 2003. An on-site chef's garden supplies dinners served—to guests only—in the restaurant, along with the basket of breakfast that's dropped off at each cottage in the morning. An A-frame-style building houses the library and features walls of windows overlooking the property's lake.

"John and I became friends many, many years ago when Taliesin Architects was building the Monona Terrace in Madison," says Dobrowolski. "I had contacted them because of the fact that we had some connections to Mr. Wright. We had gotten to be friends with the Johnsons [founders of SC Johnson in Racine]. It was kind of a circuitous route. John and I got to be pen pals, if you will. He's an interesting fellow with an interesting family." Rattenbury's wife even worked for Wright for twelve years.

When Rattenbury visited the 305-acre property that would later become Canoe Bay, the two men roamed the site to evaluate the best spot to place the cabins. Like Wright's designs, there was true intention on the part of Kelly Davis, an architect with SALA Architects in Stillwater, Minnesota, another partner in the cabins' evolution. Among Davis's restoration projects is the Donald Lovness House in Stillwater, Minnesota, designed by Wright.

Dobrowolski also visited Rattenbury at Taliesin West, in Scottsdale, Arizona, Wright's winter retreat, where many of Wright's fellows and apprentices also worked.

"John was a true Wrightian. When you see John's work, you see Wright's work," says Dobrowolski.

In recent years, the Dobrowolskis launched Escape Homes: tiny houses that can be booked on-site, or sold as built units to add to another property. They're a clear offshoot of Rattenbury's designs, with an equal focus on bringing the outdoors in, and making the home seem anything but small.

Charles and Dorothy Manson House, Wausau

Tour info: This is a private residence and not open for tours. Please respect the owners' privacy.

This 2,462-square-foot Usonian is tucked into a hilly neighborhood on Highland Park Boulevard. It's at the bottom of the hill and on the curve of a street, immediately recognizable as a Wright house.

Jonathan Leck has been hired by the most recent stewards of the house to bring it back to its original condition, including installing a new roof, updating the heating and cooling systems, and upgrading the insulation. "They searched all over the country for a Wright house," Leck says, and found it here in Northern Wisconsin. "Their taking this thing on is the best thing to have happened. We're not doing sexy stuff. It's the stuff that has to be done." Working on these structural repairs is also a homecoming for Leck, who grew up in Wausau and returned specifically to work on this project.

There have been eight families who've lived in this home over the last eighty years. One of those stewards, Donald Aucutt, coauthored *Wausau Beautiful: A Guide to Our Historic Architecture* and extensively researched the home. Charles Manson commissioned the home from Wright, and it was built between 1938 and 1941. Local brick and cypress wood comprised much of the construction. As an inheritor of his father's insurance agency, Manson's

background was also in travel and journalism. Returning home to Wausau meant settling down, in this house. Some of its unique spaces include an upstairs darkroom for Charles's photography and a very small bedroom and bath adjacent, originally designed for a live-in maid.

A fireplace in the largest room downstairs—the living room—is joined by three bedrooms, a bath, and a galley-style kitchen between one wall. A dining-room table original to the home represents the only remaining piece of Wright-designed furnishings. The rest were sold off. Unique to this Usonian was Wright's first use of perforated windows.

One of the challenges in restoring this home was recently tackled. Ten thousand locally famous Ringle Brick Company dark-burgundy bricks, just like the ones Wright used, were sourced as a complete lot. Up until 1943 these bricks were made at the Wausau company, founded by former mayor and postmaster John Ringle.

Leck has worked on many Wright homes, including the Jacobs I House in Madison and the Louis Fredrick House in Barrington, Illinois, a project that grew from six weeks to four years, a testament to how much love and care he puts into the work. For both of those projects he partnered with John Eifler, an architect also skilled in restoring Wright homes. Leck has even developed a lighting line (JPLeck Design) of sconces, floor lamps, and table lamps,

based on his own designs and those of Wright's; for example, Japanese-lantern-style Usubi lamps; Soul Lanterns (featuring cherry, walnut, red oak, or ash); near facsimiles of a floor lamp Wright designed for the 1915 Sherman Booth House; and a Taliesin floor lamp.

In 2016 the house landed a spot on the National Register of Historic Places. It is also on Wisconsin's State Register of Historic Places.

Duey and Julia Wright House, Wausau
Tour info: Open for tours Monday–Friday during business hours.

This 1,000 square foot Usonian Automatic, a half block off bustling Grand Avenue and surrounded by mature trees, is a rare example of a Wright design in the same family since it was built in 1959. But its usage has changed over the years.

First, it was a family home for Duey and Julia Wright, the owners of a local music store (Wright's Music Store on Third Street in downtown Wausau), on the 3-acre lot. They were not related to the architect. It's been reported that on move-in day they only brought their clothes, as if flipping a switch into a new lifestyle. Wright had designed all the furnishings, so there was no need to pack their dining table or beds. Fabrics and wallpapers (in the bedrooms only) were also designed by Wright and produced by F. Schumacher & Co., a fine home-goods company founded in 1889, and still in business today.

Similar to the evolution of other Wright-designed homes, this one began in two ways: with a letter from the homeowner to Wright (Julia reportedly wrote the letter); and friends who had already commissioned a Wright home (Dorothy and Charles Manson's Usonian, built in 1941, in Wausau). Wright developed two designs for the couple, and they chose this one, as it was smaller. Common materials were cement and plywood, to keep costs down, while still building a beautiful home.

On a tour of the home, it's easy to see that Wright wove music themes into the design. Many of these accents are subtle—like Wright's interpretation of Beethoven's *Fifth Symphony* in the clerestory window design, or a round kitchen window (as well as ceiling lights) representing a whole note. It's only from an aerial perspective that you might recognize the home is shaped like a quarter note.

One of the grandsons, Michael, now owns the home with his sister, Mary Kay. Michael and other family members lived in the home for seven years after Julia's 1991 passing. He serves as chief operating officer for a business run out of the home since 1998, Midwest Communications. Duke Wright, Duey and Julia's son, is the president and CEO and Mary Kay is the chief marketing officer and manages the Nashville market, while Jeffrey (Mary Kay and Michael's brother) is the company's chief sales officer. By leasing the home to the business, they were able to fund the updates. Founded in 1958, coincidentally the same year this house was built, the company manages eighty-one radio properties in nine states. Each of the four bedrooms serves as executive offices for the company's human resources, payroll, and accounting departments, and the five baths are used by employees and visitors. Three of those baths are en suite, connected to the now-offices.

"All of the original furniture designed by Wright is still owned by the family and in storage or in use currently at the house," says Michael Wright.

Wright fans are welcome to show up at the home unannounced. Becky Chapman, the company's receptionist, works at a round desk in what used to the dining room. She's armed and ready with a fact sheet about the home and loves to give short, casual tours. Sprinkled in with the decor—a mix of what an office needs to function on a day-to-day basis and some of the Wrights' family photos—are historic relics, such as a poster advertising a performance by Duke Wright and his Orchestra. There's also a famed RCA Nipper Dog statue in the entry.

From the baths' original mauve tiles—the powder room off the entry also boasts 24-karat gold wallpaper—to the built-in storage in the "bedrooms," virtually nothing has been changed. In fact, so few items have been updated that Chapman can quickly rattle those off. The upholstery on the living-room sofas is the most obvious change. In the living room, a floor-to-ceiling fireplace is joined by cushioned bench seats that can accommodate thirty, beneath the curved wall window. This is where the Wrights hosted evening music parties, says Chapman, with participants toting their instruments of choice. Eighty feet below, at the bottom of a bluff, is the Wisconsin River. Julia's books are still found in the built-ins. When she and her husband lived here, the library "would have had a baby grand piano and a black chaise lounge," says Chapman.

Wright carefully considered the site's existing trees and their placement when drawing up plans for the house, which boasts an eye-catching pyramidal hipped roof and, like other Usonians, radiant floor heating to keep away the chill of Northern Wisconsin winters. (Forced air and radiant heating were later installed.)

There were four elements Wright wanted to incorporate: wood, glass, concrete, and plaster. Walls and built-ins were crafted from rare Philippine mahogany. So well made was the kitchen that everything is original (including the built-in blender)—although, to be fair, no one is cooking for a family now, as before. The kitchen is primarily used for employees' lunches and snacks. Despite a $40,000 quote, the home ended up costing three times more than that.

There is only one other Usonian Automatic design, and that is in Fox Point: the Albert and Edith Adelman House. How this Usonian differs is that it features carpeting (except for the entryway and kitchen), plastered ceilings, a three-stall carport (most Wright homes have room for one car, maybe two), and a partial basement.

This home also has the acclaim of being the last private residence Wright designed before his 1959 death. Unfortunately, he never got to see the design through to its completion. At that time, he was occupied with the Guggenheim Museum in New York City. John Howe and John deKoven Hill worked on the plans for this home, which was put on the National Register of Historic Places in 1998.

The Stewart Inn, Wausau
Tour info: Open for overnight stays year-round. stewartinn.com

Innkeepers Randy and Sara Bangs knew immediately, the first time they saw this historic property, that they wanted to be its next stewards. With experience managing other bed-and-breakfasts throughout Wisconsin, visiting or living in Wausau wasn't ever on their radar, but on a research trip they fell in love with this small town for its cultural arts, philanthropy, and, more importantly, historic preservation.

That includes this five-room B&B, referred to as the Stewart Inn, and located on Grant Street near downtown Wausau. In their B&B search, the Bangs had three items on their wish

list: the ability to provide a great stay; good food; and fun things to do nearby. This inn and the surrounding neighborhood met all three, including its proximity to three microbreweries, a distillery, two art museums, a cheese shop, the state's largest continuously operated bookstore, and the Grand Theater.

They bought the inn in 2016 and reopened in early 2017. It had been closed for five years prior, but had functioned as a B&B since the late 1980s.

Designed by George Maher—known for his Prairie-style architecture, being a founder of the Chicago Arts and Crafts Society, and a fellow draftsman of Wright's at the Chicago office of architect Joseph Silsbee—in 1906, it was originally a private residence. The Hiram C. and Irene Stewart House was built for a lumber baron and his wife who relocated from Bay City, Michigan, and raised two children in the home. It took two years to build the house, and the family only stayed until 1913, departing for Pasadena, California, when flooding affected old-growth forests and, ultimately, the lumber industry. Unfortunately, in 1926, Maher died of suicide.

Maher worked with Wright in the early 1890s, and that influence is obvious on a tour of this B&B. However, "Maher was less organic than Wright," says Randy Bangs. As a nod to Maher's Arts and Crafts roots, the couple has decorated with Arts and Crafts furnishings and decor whenever possible. But there's another reason, too. "Arts and Crafts architecture has universal appeal across the generations," says Bangs. It's unlike Victorian architecture, which might not find fans among younger guests, or the way older guests might scoff at Midcentury Modern architecture.

Although most of Maher's designs—from residential commissions to Northwestern University's original Patten Gymnasium and Swift Hall of Engineering—reside in Chicago or the North Shore suburbs, he did design several homes in Wausau. He also designed the Marathon

County Historical Society's current home; Wausau's former library, later torn down; and six private Wausau homes. This inn was Wausau's first property on the National Register of Historic Places.

There are six fireplaces: one each in the downstairs living room, the library, and the third floor; and three in the guest rooms, which are all on the second floor. The second-floor Sheldon Room is the largest, and was a former sitting room. Just like years ago, today's guests arrive through the inn to the large, boxy foyer cloaked in mahogany. The adjacent entrance was originally designed as a carriage entrance, and a powder room nearby allowed guests to freshen up after the long journey. The foyer's built-in bench and red tiling (much like Wright's beloved Cherokee Red) are joined by original stained-glass windows designed by Giannini and Hilgart, both Chicago artisans who frequently worked with Wright.

Next, guests walk up a few granite steps into the open-layout living room and dining room, where breakfast is served each morning. A coffered ceiling cultivates a cozy vibe, and light pours through stained-glass windows. The living room's window seat is a favorite resting spot for the couple's German longhaired pointer Buster. Arts and Crafts–style seating surrounds the mosaic fireplace, including Stickley-style quarter-sawn oak sofas with leather cushions, and a stained-glass, tulip-motif chandelier overhead casting a soft glow. Suspended just above the dining-room table hangs another light fixture true to the period, housing stained-glass panels in its round shape, and with

beaded fringe beneath. This was a collaboration between Giannini and Hilgart and Willy Lau (a lighting designer in Chicago who also created metalwork for the inn's sconces and other chandeliers).

What was once Stewart's office is now the inn's library, which features stucco walls, quarter-sawn oak bookcases, and an Arts and Crafts–style brick fireplace. An original chandelier (once a cigar ventilator) as well as sconces remain.

"George Maher was known for his Motif Rhythm theory," explains Bangs, "the concept that you would take an architectural design and mirror it throughout the house." At the Stewart Inn, the two motifs he employed are a tripartite (or segmental) arch and tulips.

Original sinks are in each of the guest rooms' en suite baths, and the quarter-sawn oak floors are also original. Included with rates is morning breakfast—an elaborate three-course meal prepared by Randy—and an evening wine reception.

Wright and Like Tour
wrightinwisconsin.org

Each June or July, Wright in Wisconsin, an organization whose overarching goal is to promote, protect, and preserve the heritage of Frank Lloyd Wright, hosts a tour that is a coveted experience for Wright fans. Tickets typically go on sale beginning in the spring. This is when you can walk inside a handful of private homes not normally open to the public. It's an artful mix of Wright homes and others designed by architects in the spirit of Wright; hence, the tour's name. Many of the Wright-like homes were designed by members of the Taliesin Fellowship, a group of architect apprentices, and architectural designers who worked closely with Wright and employed his principles of organic architecture.

For example, the 2015 Wright and Like Tour featured the Mary Lescohier and Louise Kloepper House (1963) by Wright apprentice William Wesley Peters and Taliesin Associated Architects, along with the Stewart and Jacqueline Macaulay House (1963) by apprentice

John Howe. Both are in Madison. Regarding the Macaulay House, "One cannot mistake it for anything other than [being designed] by John Howe," says George Hall, Wright in Wisconsin's interim treasurer and past president. "Howe, for several decades, was 'the pencil in Wright's hand.'"

On occasion, the homeowners themselves are your guide (or trained volunteer docents) as they show you around these works of art that also happen to be their private home. There are opportunities to ask questions and experience what it's like to be inside a Wright-designed residence (or a Wright-like abode) for a spell. It's one thing to read about these homes and another to view photos. But standing in a living room and admiring Wright's handicraft, or how he inspired another architect, is at a whole other level.

In 2022—the tour's twenty-third season—Wright and Like descended upon Madison and Middleton, visiting four Wright residences: two by Wright apprentices, and another two by a Wright-inspired architectural designer and an architect, all under the theme of Wright or Marshall Erdman prefabs. Here's a snapshot of three of the eight homes that were featured.

The Robert M. Lamp House (1903) in downtown Madison, one block off the Capitol Square, is Wright's oldest remaining Madison structure. He designed this for a childhood friend. Although currently rented out to UW–Madison students, it's the subject of a preservation and redevelopment project, says Hall. "Wright's only family home was [just] a few blocks away from Lamp. From the roof deck, the house had views of Lake Monona and Lake Mendota [of which a partial view remains today], as well as the State Capitol Building a block away."

The Eric Vogelman House (1981) was constructed by Vogelman (along with one of his brothers) to be his personal residence. He now lives in Colorado, where he practices architecture. "The home contains many design principles found in Wright's home and studio out in Spring Green," says Hall.

Jacobs II (1948) was built in what is now Middleton for the Jacobs family, as a larger country home, after Wright designed their first house on the west side of Madison. The homeowners enjoy growing fruits and vegetables on the site, just as the Jacobses did, and have further added to their art-sculpture garden over the years.

Hall, a retired urban planner, and Traci Schnell, a historic-preservation consultant, and Wright in Wisconsin office administrator Bill Swan, tirelessly planned the tour. "It takes a fair amount of research to find suitable houses, before approaching owners," says Hall, "and with many of the apprentice and 'like' architect homes approaching fifty or sixty years old, we're losing them as tear-downs." This is why it's important to highlight even the homes inspired by Wright, as they may not be on the national or state historic registers, and in danger of being razed or altered from their original state.

"Tours are geographically organized, rotating among several areas around the state where there are concentrations of Wright buildings, apprentice houses, or homes by 'like' architects," says Hall. "Their popularity occasionally draws guests from nearby states as well as the coasts and foreign countries. Our office has, over the years, assisted groups of foreign architects who visit the United States."

In 2019—later taking 2020 and 2021 off, due to COVID-19 pandemic—the tour expanded to Two Rivers, Oostburg, and Manitowoc for the first time, touring eight homes that included Wright's Bernard and Fern Schwartz House ("Still Bend"), built in 1940 in Two Rivers, and others designed by John Bloodgood Schuster, who worked closely with Russell Barr Williamson. Williamson was a well-known and close associate of Wright's.

These aren't all historic homes, which is part of the allure. On the abovementioned tour, a home designed in 2017 by Racine architect Ken Dahlin was included, because it's modeled after Wright's Usonian designs.

Whether you're a practicing architect or the kind of person who trolls home-design websites, this tour is one to add to your bucket list.

Frank Lloyd Wright Trail

If you're driving along the highway in Southern Wisconsin, a series of brown metal signs along the roadside may catch your eye. These aren't advising you of the speed limit or notifying you of food and gas options at the next exit. They're telling you that you're on the Frank Lloyd Wright Trail.

Created in 2017, the trail weaves through nine counties, connecting nine sites. From the southeastern part of the state, one would begin in Racine County, with SC Johnson's Administration Building and Research Tower, and Wingspread, and then continue through Milwaukee, Madison, and Spring Green, ending at A. D. German Warehouse in Richland Center. That last stop also happens to be the town where Wright was born. While there is no official passport, motorists are encouraged to peruse a page on Travel Wisconsin's website that lays out the nine sites in geographical sequence.

Of course, the direction of this trail can also be reversed, to begin in Richland Center and end in Racine County. And dropping by sites on the trail but not completing the entire trail is also encouraged.

In Milwaukee, the trail features the Burnham Block, where six American System-Built Homes either restored or in the process of being restored sit proudly on a South Side block. These were designed for the working class, and while only around twenty were ultimately built, Wright created more than 900 drawings. For the project, Wright partnered with developer Arthur Richards and Wright's assistant, Russell Barr Williamson. It ended when Wright sued Richards, ultimately canceling the project forever.

Next, it's a smooth sail down I-94 West to downtown Madison, where Monona Terrace sits proudly alongside Lake Mendota. Although not built until 1997, it was based on Wright's designs created during the 1930s. Today Monona Terrace is a popular site for weddings and also hosts conferences. On the west side of Madison, Wright's boyhood church—the First Unitarian Society Meeting House—is of his own design and was built in 1951, just eight years before his death. And then, finally, it's on to Taliesin, Wright's summer estate during his adult years, but also where he was raised by an extended family of Unitarians. In Welsh, his family's native language, *Taliesin* means "shining brow." Despite three tragic fires, in 1914, 1925, and 1952, it's one of the state's most popular tourism sites and attracts visitors from around the globe.

The final two stops on the trail, if one departed from Racine County, are the Wyoming Valley School Cultural Arts Center in Spring Green (a 1956 school that's now an art gallery and events center) and the A. D. German Warehouse in Richland Center (a four-story warehouse with cast concrete motifs completed in 1921, currently under restoration to become a multipurpose community building with a theater, eateries, and other small businesses).

INDEX

PHOTO CREDITS

Pages 1–4: The Kubala Washatko Architects
Page 5: JMKE Photography
Pages 6–8: Mark Hertzberg
Pages 10–11: Robert Hartmann
Pages 12–15: Robert Hartmann
Page 16: Visit Milwaukee
Pages 18–20: Nicholas Hayes
Pages 21–24: Will Skaggs
Pages 26–28: Mark Hertzberg
Pages 29–31: Robert Hartmann
Pages 33–36: Mark Hertzberg
Pages 39–41: Mark Hertzberg
Pages 42–44: Mark Hertzberg
Page 45: Travel Wisconsin
Page 46: Wingspread
Page 47: Travel Wisconsin
Page 48–49: Wingspread
Pages 51–53: Mark Hertzberg
Pages 56–57: Mark Hertzberg
Pages 59–63: VISIT Lake Geneva
Pages 65–67: Mark Hertzberg
Page 68: Travel Wisconsin
Page 69: Alison Long
Page 70: First Unitarian Society of Madison
Pages 72–73: David Heald
Page 74: Kristine Hansen
Pages 76–77: John W. Moore
Page 78: Mark Hertzberg
Pages 80–84: Eliot Butler
Page 85: Monona Terrace Community and Convention Center
Page 86: Brittany Klemm
Page 87: Errin Hiltbrand
Page 88: Todd Brei
Page 89: Jared Hamilton Thrive Photography & Video
Page 90: Spring Valley Inn
Pages 91–93: Taliesin
Pages 94–95: Travel Wisconsin
Page 97: Travel Wisconsin

Pages 99–101: Wyoming Valley Inc.
Page 102: Travel Wisconsin
Pages 103–108: Andrew Pielage and Schwartz House/Still Bend
Pages 109–112: Kelly Radandt
Pages 113–114: Robert Hartmann
Page 115: Mary Arnold
Page 116: Mark Hertzberg
Page 117: Wisconsin Dells Visitor and Convention Bureau
Pages 119–123: Kit Hogan
Pags 124–125: Wisconsin Dells Visitor and Convention Bureau
Pages 127–130: Canoe Bay
Pages 131–132: Irina Hynes
Page 133: Tyler J Aug
Pages 134–138: Dave Kallaway
Pages 139–144: The Stewart Inn
Pages 145–148: George Hall
Page 149: Mark Hertzberg

ACKNOWLEDGMENTS

Without the genius architect there would be no book. There would also be a lot less for us Wright fans to talk about. Now, with this book shipped off to my editor, I feel as if I've gained entrance into an amazing club of Wright aficionados. You are a warm, friendly, and engaging bunch! I have many Wright experts to thank for answering my many emails and phone calls.

Minerva Montooth, for sharing your memories of Mr. Wright and Olgivanna, and inviting me for tea at your apartment on the Taliesin estate. Keiran Murphy for reviewing the timeline. Mary Jane Hamilton for sharing your A. B. Groves Building Co. House research. Mark Hertzberg, who I actually met years earlier as a newsroom intern at the *Journal Times* in Racine, Wisconsin, when he was the photography director, but got to know better through the course of this project. You skillfully took me under your wing and introduced me to all the right people in order to do this book justice. John Eifler, you didn't hesitate to connect me to your clients, and I would be wealthy if I earned even a dollar for every time your name came up in the course of doing interviews around the state. Nicholas Hayes, for sharing your experiences—the good and the bad—of living in a Frank Lloyd Wright–designed house, and taking the time on a Friday afternoon to linger over your homemade chai is not an experience I take for granted. Your input about American System-Built Homes and the Munkwitz Apartments was also helpful. Bob Hartmann, the photos, stories, and connections you offered could only have come from one of the biggest Wright fans I know. Bill Martinelli, your name came up repeatedly as I talked to Wright conservationists, and when we finally met at the Seth Peterson Cottage and Jacobs I House, I could see why: Your passion for saving Wright's works is admirable. Each manager at a Wright site who either invited me on a group tour and stayed patiently after to answer all of my questions, or met me after hours for a private tour, thank you. For each steward of a Frank Lloyd Wright–designed house who opened your literal door to me and let me in, whether it was a rainy or a sunny day, and whether my deadline was way off in the future or, gasp, in two weeks. I never felt anything less than cozy and comfortable in your homes, which I think has as much to say about how you've decorated the interiors as it does about Wright's intentions. I'm a city girl, and hearing the birds chirp again—proof he was correct about blending into the landscape—was the balm I didn't know I needed.

Before I began work on this book I'd considered myself a Wright aficionado, having written and published numerous articles about his projects and visited many of his sites around the country. Little did I know there was so much more to learn! I am forever grateful to the authors of these books for allowing me to settle in at night, after a day of writing, with a front-row seat to the research you've already done. This includes John Gurda's *New World Odyssey: Annunciation Greek Orthodox Church and Frank Lloyd Wright*; Mark Hertzberg's *Wright in Racine: The Architect's Vision for One American City*, *Frank Lloyd Wright's Hardy House*, *Frank Lloyd Wright's SC Johnson Research Tower*, and *Frank Lloyd Wright's Penwern: A Summer Estate*; Nicholas D. Hayes's *Frank Lloyd Wright's Forgotten House: How an Omission*

Transformed the Architect's Legacy; and Kristin Visser and John Eifler's *Frank Lloyd Wright's Seth Peterson Cottage: Rescuing a Lost Masterwork.*

To friends and family who send me links to anything published on the Internet about Frank Lloyd Wright, thank you. Or, the thoughtful questions you've asked (I'm looking at you, Bob!) that got me out of my own way and helped frame this book's narrative. A writer is nothing without her editors, and I thank my editors at Realtor.com, Fodor's guidebooks, ArchitecturalDigest.com, *Midwest Living* magazine, and *Milwaukee* magazine, for assigning me stories about Frank Lloyd Wright over the years. Each of those articles may be in the distant past, but the information I retained was like gold as I worked on this book. Amy Lyons, my delightful book editor, you know just the right things to say when I'm freaking out on the other end. I'm glad you saw the potential in this book and helped shape it into its current form.

And, finally, I would be remiss if I didn't mention my Wright travel partner in crime, Tony Walczak, who shared many nights with me in Wright's homes, and being the ferocious reader that he is, probably knows as much, if not more, about Mr. Wright than I do.

ABOUT THE AUTHOR

Based in Milwaukee, Wisconsin, **Kristine Hansen** grew up in Northern Illinois and makes it a point to visit as many Wright sites as she can. She's also the author of *Wisconsin Cheese Cookbook: Creamy, Cheesy, Sweet, and Savory Recipes from the State's Best Creameries* and *Wisconsin Farms and Farmers Markets: Tours, Trails, and Attractions*, and contributes to Architectural Digest.com, *Milwaukee Magazine*, TravelandLeisure.com, and Realtor.com about architecture and design.